The Left Hand
of God

CONFRONTATION BOOKS
William H. Lazareth, Editor

Ecological Renewal by Paul E. Lutz and H. Paul Santmire

Doing Theology in a Revolutionary Situation by José Míguez
Bonino

THE LEFT HAND
OF GOD

Essays on Discipleship and Patriotism

Edited by
WILLIAM H. LAZARETH

with contributions by

GERHARD A. KRODEL
WILLIAM H. LAZARETH
CLARENCE L. LEE
OLIVER K. OLSON

FORTRESS PRESS
Philadelphia

Library of Congress Catalog Card Number 75-36457

ISBN 0-8006-1452-6

5413L75   Printed in U.S.A.   1-1452

Contents

Contents

Editor's Foreword

Confrontation Books aim to confront the involved reader with the cross of Christ amid the crossroads of life. Confrontations are central to Christianity: both at the cross, for the content of Christian faith, and at the crossroads, for the context of Christian love. To enable responsible persons to confront both life in Christ and Christ in life is the dialectical hallmark of authentic Christian theology.

Paul sharply contrasts two opposing types of theology: that of the contemplation of heaven and that of confrontation in the world. Theology can describe either our search for God or God's search for us. The choice determines the method.

If our basic problem is considered to be our ignorance as finite creatures, then knowledge of God may properly be sought through rational speculation. If, rather, our essential dilemma is confessed to be our idolatry as proud and disobedient sinners, then knowledge of God can be achieved only through God's gracious self-revelation. Paul's gospel was regarded as scandalous by the religious people of his day precisely because he rejected human-centered contemplation in the name of Christ-centered confrontation: "When the time had fully come, God sent forth his Son. . . . Formerly, when you did not know God, you were in bondage to beings that by nature are not gods, but now . . . you have come to know God, or rather to be known by God" (Gal. 4:8–9).

Ours is therefore a *theology of worldly confrontation*: "God was in Christ reconciling the world to himself." No biblical theme is more promising for Christian renewal than the liberating gospel and God's ministry of reconciliation, grounded in Christ's cross and proclaimed by Christ's church. In opposition to the rash of recent religious fads, the hidden lordship of the crucified Christ still constitutes the heart of the apostolic good news.

In a frightened and confused age, "Christ-figures" and "redemptive movements" rise and fall almost weekly. They pass by in dizzying succession in response to the futile attempts to match our technological prowess in a shrinking world with some commensurate form of ideological universalism. However, the cross of the one unique Christ—Jesus of Nazareth—remains faith's unswerving answer to the institutional church's present "identity crisis": its seeming inability to become lovingly *identified with* the world without also becoming faithlessly *identical to* the world. Our suffering theology is no substitute for God's "suffering servant." We need to recapture that paradoxical unity of universality and particularity which undergirds Paul's gospel of God's reconciling work in Jesus of Nazareth, the Second Adam who incorporates a new humanity into a new covenant with life's Lord.

Ours is also an *ethic of worldly confrontation*: "As you did it to one of the least of these my brethren, you did it to me." Apathetic Christians need to be reminded that Christ-centered reconciliation must always be viewed in the light of God's righteousness and judgment. Christian reconciliation in an evil world has nothing to do with either noncommittal neutrality or uninvolved appeasement. While Jesus surely died for all men, he also lived especially for some—the poor, the weak, the dispossessed, "the least of these my brethren." The church, as the reconciling body of the risen Christ, is called to minister likewise.

Confrontation Books, committed to each one's personal confrontation with the cross of Christ amid the crossroads of life, will engage in down-to-earth theology in fidelity to a down-to-earth Lord. Readers are invited to think theologically (in depth before God) about the actual problems of life that confront them daily.

Our age, especially, challenges Christian theology to authenticate itself by responding humanely to the host of medical, political, racial, and military threats and opportunities facing humanity. In Confrontation Books, therefore, ecumenical authors of various churches, races, nationalities, and professions will seek to develop current Christian life-styles by confronting controversial secular problems with biblical insights and theological affirmations of faith—e.g., pollution, heroin, revolution, and nuclear warfare illumined by the person as God's image, Christ as man's liberator, the church as sign of the world's unity, and the kingdom as God's reign among men.

We seek thereby to demonstrate the truth of Luther's words, "Not reading and speculation, but living, dying, and being condemned makes a real theologian."

The American Revolution was a struggle for human rights grounded in the sovereign law of God. At a time when only five percent of the colonists were church members committed to the Christian gospel, moral justification for the War of Independence was based on the law of God the Creator.

In testimony to God's universal law, the American Revolution was a state of mind long before it became a state of war. Preceding and prompting the military battles was the colonists' fervent conviction that their God-given human rights were being violated. They believed that they were "endowed by their Creator with certain inalienable rights" (Declaration of Independence). They experienced the abrogation of these rights by civil laws and political policies that were unjust to persons created by a just God.

Prophetic religion provides a moral sanction for the just exercise of political power. Governments and laws will not long be obeyed if citizens created in God's image consider them to be inherently unjust. There has been universal testimony among Christians and non-Christians alike to a "higher law" that the state serves. Behind and beyond the civil laws of society stand the moral "laws of nature and of nature's God" (Declaration of Independence).

Hence, the practice of "taxation without representation" may have been technically legal according to English parliamentary law. The colonists still viewed it as morally unjust according to society's "higher law." Although God's justice is hard for theologians to define, human injustice is easy for oppressed citizens to describe.

Even so canny a political realist as John Adams acknowledged that it was basically religious convictions that inspired the revolutionary actions of the colonists. The English government was no longer considered the legitimate custodian of human rights or the valid representative of divine justice. Adams therefore identified "the real American Revolution" as the spiritual one that took place prior to the battlefields within the hearts of the people:

> What do we mean by the American Revolution? Do we mean the American war? The Revolution was effected before the war commenced. The Revolution was in the minds and hearts of the people; *a change in their religious sentiments of their duties and obligations.* . . .
>
> The people of America had been educated in an habitual affection for England as their mother country; and while they thought her a kind and tender parent (erroneously enough, however, for she never was such a mother), no affection could be more sincere. But when they found her a cruel beldam [hag], willing like Lady Macbeth to "dash their brains out," it is no wonder if their filial affections ceased, and were changed into indignation and horror.
>
> This radical change in the principles, opinions, sentiments and affections of the people was the real American Revolution. (*Letter to Hezekiah Niles,* 1818, emphasis added)

As American Lutherans, the authors of this volume are especially interested in the impact of this "real Revolution" on the political role of their fellow believers in the eighteenth century. After all, the American Revolution was a test case for the commitment of Lutheran colonists to the law of God the Creator which sanctioned "liberty and justice for all." Both illustrative and instructive are the very different responses of the four pastors—father and three sons—who then represented the leading Lutheran family in the colonies.[1]

The outbreak of hostilities in 1776 found the aged "patriarch of American Lutheranism," Henry Melchior Muhlenberg, preparing for retirement. He had completed over three decades of ministry as a saddleback preacher and church organizer. Meanwhile his three sons were actively serving congregations in different colonies: Peter in Virginia, Frederick in New York, and Henry Ernest in Pennsylvania. Although the Muhlenbergs grew up in the same home and church, their responses ranged from prudent neutrality to militant support of the revolution.

Henry Melchior Muhlenberg was officially neutral toward the war. True to his Pietistic heritage from Halle, Germany, the head of the Muhlenberg clan remained aloof from politics as a minister of the gospel. He was naturally conservative in temperament, and respected the authority of the English crown.

Furthermore, he was grateful for the government's protection of the colonists and his missionary work among them. He had close relations with London's Society for Preaching Christian Knowledge and lauded the "inestimable blessings" of the "mild and blessed government" of Great Britain. He continued to pray publicly for King George until the war's opening shots at Lexington and Concord.

Throughout the struggles for independence, Henry Melchior was plagued by divided loyalties. At first he viewed the revolution as divine punishment on both unfaithful peoples. "God, who rules over all things," he wrote in June 1775, "is using the motherland as a rod for America; then when the divine purpose is achieved and the rod is worn out, it will be cast away."

Gradually, however, Henry Melchior's official neutrality was conditioned by a growing sympathy for the cause of the colonies. He hoped for a negotiated settlement of the colonists' justifiable grievances. Mother England, by violating American liberties, was unjustly trying to be "disciplinarian and execu-

1. Biographical details and documented quotations are taken from Paul A. Wallace, *The Muhlenbergs of Pennsylvania* (Philadelphia: University of Pennsylvania Press, 1950).

tioner over her own daughter." While he would continue to deplore "this unnatural and inhuman war, he could also privately counsel his son-in-law in March 1776, "The young people are right in fighting for their God-given native liberty." Following the signing of the Declaration of Independence, he made a cryptic entry in his journal on July 4, 1776, "The end will show who played the right tune."

A few months later, as life became more dangerous in Philadelphia, Henry Melchior fled with his wife to the countryside. He explained his flight in a personal letter:

> Robbed of my former protection, old and cast aside, unwilling to change my oath of allegiance nor yet to be a sacrifice to anarchy at the hands of the angry mob, I retired . . . to a little country place of 7 acres [at Trappe, Pennsylvania] . . . intended for poor, superannuated Lutheran preachers or poor widows, in the hope of having a quiet, retired life.

Most kindred in spirit to his apolitical father was the youngest of the three Muhlenberg sons, Henry Ernest. A learned preacher and scholar, Henry Ernest achieved honors in Lancaster, Pennsylvania. He was elected a member of the American Philosophical Society and named the first principal of Franklin College.

Henry Ernest also became internationally known as a leading botanist, emulating his Swedish mentor and earning the title of "the American Linnaeus." His botanical scholarship even merited the appreciative notice of Thomas Jefferson:

> I embrace with pleasure this occasion of assuring you that I have had long and much gratification in observing the distinguished part you have borne in making known to the literary world the treasures of our own country, and I tender to you the sentiments of my high respect and esteem.

Of special interest to us, however, is the fact that Henry Ernest diligently carried out his religious and scientific pursuits while virtually oblivious to the turmoil and suffering of the American Revolution. He was a political quietist whose religious spirit was far less conscious of God's presence in history than in nature. He once confessed:

And I have felt
A Presence that disturbs me with joy
Of elevated thoughts; a sense sublime
Of something far more deeply interfused,
Whose dwelling is the light of setting suns
And the round ocean and the living air.

A second son, Peter Gabriel, gained widespread fame as a militant supporter of the revolutionary cause. In January 1776, while still an ordained clergyman, he secretly accepted a colonel's commission in the army of Virginia. The twenty-nine-year-old pastor's dramatic leave-taking of his congregation at Woodstock, Virginia, was destined to become a classic in American patriotic folklore.

Peter's great-nephew, Henry A. Muhlenberg, later recounted one romanticized version of the event in his *Life of Major General Peter Muhlenberg of the Revolutionary Army* (1849):

> He ascended the pulpit, his tall form arrayed in full uniform, over which his gown, the symbol of his holy calling, was thrown. . . . After recapitulating, in words that aroused the coldest, the story of their sufferings and their wrongs, and telling them of the sacred character of the struggle in which he had unsheathed his sword, and for which he had left the altar he had vowed to serve, he said that "in the language of Holy Writ, there was a time for all things, a time to preach and a time to pray, but those times had passed away;" and in a voice that re-echoed through the church like a trumpet-blast, "that there was a time to fight, and that time had now come!"
>
> The sermon finished, he pronounced the benediction. . . . Deliberately putting off the gown, which had thus far covered his martial figure, he stood before them a girded warrior; and descending from the pulpit, ordered the drums at the churchdoor to beat for recruits.

Much to Father Muhlenberg's dismay, Peter never returned to the parish ministry. Following his fiery sermon, a few hundred men enlisted immediately in his 8th Virginia Regiment. That action initiated a notable military career in the Continental Army. He eventually rose to the rank of major general under the command of George Washington. After the war, Peter entered political affairs and was elected vice-president of Pennsylvania. At the national level, he served as a member of the House of Representatives in the First, Third, and Sixth Congresses, and finally became a member of the United States Senate. A republican of the spirit of Jefferson, Peter championed human rights and constitutional government.

The third Muhlenberg son, Frederick Augustus, found that his sympathies for political independence also drew him out of the ministry. Shunning the military however, he went into political life. He and his family fled from their New York parish to Pennsylvania after the British shelled and occupied the city in late 1775 and 1776. Though opposed to the Tories, Frederick continued to serve as pastor of a number of rural congregations outside Philadelphia. After the war, he left the pastorate and was elected one of Pennsylvania's three delegates to the Continental Congress. On hearing the surprising news, Frederick's distraught father was moved to enter in his journal the words of Jesus in the Lord's Prayer, "Lead us not into temptation."

Frederick became a powerful figure in Pennsylvania politics for the rest of his life. After serving as speaker of the Pennsylvania Assembly from Philadelphia, he was elected president of the Council of Censors which revised the Pennsylvania Constitution. He also represented his electorate nationally in the first four Congresses of the House of Representatives, serving as speaker in the First and the Third. He was a conservative Federalist who worked hard to protect the gains of the revolution in institutional structures that could endure the tests of time.

Highly illuminating for our survey is the heated exchange that took place between Frederick and Peter in 1776 shortly after Peter had publicly traded his preacher's gown for a military uniform. Frederick condemned Peter's action in a letter to their other brother, Henry Ernest, who, in turn, shared Frederick's letter with Peter. That set the stage for the brothers' direct confrontation, during which Peter's churchmanship and Frederick's patriotism were both impugned by each other. Here are some excerpts from their correspondence:

Peter: I am a clergyman, it is true, but I am a member of society as well as the poorest layman, and my liberty is as dear to me as to any man. Shall I then sit still and enjoy myself at home when the best blood of the continent is spilling? Heaven forbid it!

Frederick: You do not know me. I believe I have always been, and still am, as firm in our American cause as you are, even though I am not a colonel marching to the field.

Peter: I am called by my country, in its defence. The cause is just and noble. Were I a bishop, even a Lutheran one, I should obey without hesitation. And so far am I from thinking that I act wrong, I am convinced it is my duty so to do, and duty I owe to God and my country.

Frederick: I think you are wrong in trying to be both soldier and preacher together. Be either one or the other. No man can serve two masters. I have long had some doubts of my own. I recognize well my unfitness as a preacher . . . I incline to think a preacher can with good conscience resign his office and step into another calling. You think a man can be both preacher and colonel at the same time. How different are our ways of thinking!

Radical differences in "ways of thinking" among all the Muhlenbergs demonstrate the necessity of some serious Lutheran self-examination. Which, if any, of the pastors properly represented Lutheran doctrine? How were such opposing reactions possible? What may have been the impact on them of Luther and the Reformation, of the Christian tradition in medieval and early church life, and of the normative authority of the Old and New Testaments themselves?

The authors of this interdisciplinary inquiry have served as professors at the Lutheran Theological Seminary at Philadelphia. In the course of our work, we have daily passed by both the campus statue of the preaching Henry Melchior and the library display of Peter's discarded ministerial gown. In this volume we must also theologically bypass the political and military ethics of the two most famous Muhlenbergs. Neither privatistic separation (Henry Melchior) nor patriotic identification (Peter) of church and state can claim to be authentically Lutheran.

In the aftermath of Vietnam, Selma, and Watergate, the commemoration of the American Bicentennial provides an appropriate occasion for both repentance and rededication. Let it be said clearly for the "mutual conversation and consolation" of the faithful: Too many American Lutherans have not yet done their fair share in securing "liberty and justice for all." In the hindsight of history, must we not confess that too many of us have simply repeated the political and military failures of our eighteenth century forefathers?

We now have the opportunity to renew our pledge of dual allegiance both as Christians (first) and as Americans (second). A chief result of the Lutheran Reformation was the gaining of evangelical clarity on what to render to God and what to render to Caesar. Therefore our theological tradition still has an important contribution to make to America's pluralistic dialogue ahead.

Sharing that conviction, the authors offer an American Lutheran witness to the biblical view of God's twofold rule of humanity (doctrine of the Two Kingdoms). We affirm that all persons are created as citizens of God's earthly kingdom, but only some are then redeemed as saints in God's heavenly kingdom. We enter God's earthly kingdom by birth; we are born again into God's heavenly kingdom by grace through faith alone.

The Triune Lord rules both kingdoms simultaneously: with his powerful "left hand" through the universal law of creation, and with his merciful "right hand" through the saving gospel of redemption. Complementing God's mission as Redeemer and Sanctifier for our eternal righteousness is his ongoing work as Creator and Judge for our civil righteousness. That activity of the "left hand" of God—justice, freedom, and peace—constitutes our chief concern in political and military ethics.

The reality of God's "left hand" lordship in public affairs may appear remote in our age of privatized religiosity. Current philosophy declares, "Religion is what the individual does with his solitariness" (Whitehead). Constitutional law decrees, "Religion is essentially a private matter" (Burger). Church leaders give credibility to such secularized views when they limit their religious ministry to securing "decisions for Christ," and restrict their ethical guidance to condemnations of "dirty politics." When church members warn their pastors to "stick to religion," the unspoken assumption is that religion has to do with nothing more than "saving souls."

The Bible affirms rather that the Triune God rules all of life. Therefore our discipleship includes our patriotism; it is always personal but never merely private. Our "God" is far too small if he is not confessed daily as the Lord of his created world, as well as the Savior of his redeemed church.

Christians can best observe America's Bicentennial by advocating and serving the God of justice in public affairs. We will do so in obedient gratitude for the gracious gift of Jesus Christ. As disciples in a heavenly kingdom, we are called to be the priests who carry out God's "right hand" rule of personal love. As patriots in an earthly kingdom, we are also empowered to be the prophets who advocate God's "left hand" rule of social justice. In relating our patriotism to our discipleship, we affirm that the Triune God in whom we trust is gloriously ambidextrous.

Philadelphia, Pennsylvania   WILLIAM H. LAZARETH
XVII Pentecost, 1975

Oliver K. Olson

The Revolution and
the Reformation

LUTHERANS AND THE BICENTENNIAL

American Amnesia

The kind of strenuous remembering we should be doing for the Bicentennial as the first step in planning for the future has become difficult for peculiarly American reasons. We have confused hoping for a better future with stamping out the memory of the past. Schoolchildren in Spain, in France, in Germany, in England, are told that they live in an old civilization and that Americans live in a new one. America agrees; the official point of view, floating there above the sand near that peculiar pyramid on the dollar is that we constitute *a new order of the ages*.

Those who joined America after the Revolution sensed it as soon as they reached Ellis Island. The old relationships to soil, to blood, it was clear, were to be replaced by allegiance to the new order. Our duty as new people is to be Americans *regardless* of national origin, or race.

Consider Theodore Roosevelt. The hordes of immigrants, he thought, would construct communities to guard the old ways. And he mounted a campaign against "hyphenated Americans." No more Polish-Americans, no Italian-Americans, no Swedish-Americans. Just Americans.

And a million fretful children were kept in from recess for speaking German, or Danish, or Norwegian, or were kept from other means for retaining an un-American past. A million immigrant mothers were bewildered when those children, growing,

1

showed contempt for the past. And the historical identity which would have been theirs in another time, another place, was lost.

Perhaps if we are careful never to forget the anguish and loss of the *black* immigrants, incomparably greater than for the others, we can yet borrow from them a symbol. The "X" which black Malcolm pressed to himself in the place of a surname which would have related him to a specific soil and a particular stream of blood, may serve as symbol for all the memories America took away.

Mr. Roosevelt and his schoolmarms were right, of course. Rulers must unite. Historical memories are dangerous. We could keep the recipes for sauerkraut and the techniques for painting Easter eggs in a quaint ethnic manner; we could not cherish the important memories, lest we build, side by side, a series of warring communities as in the Balkans. The awesome, oyster-like power of America to *assimilate* is nowhere so powerfully demonstrated as when we think it quite natural to read in the paper that some legal precedent has been broken "for the first time since Charles II." The same is true when we accept it as natural that children are taught Shakespeare or we raise children with the help of Mother Goose. We have become, somehow, Englishmen. Perhaps what we have got is more than what we lost.

But that great "X" must haunt us. In May 1975, Alexander Woodside of Harvard printed a striking diagnosis in *The New York Times*. "The United States," he said, "is probably the contemporary world's purest example of a society which is perpetually trying to abolish history, to avoid thinking in historical terms, to associate dynamism with premeditated amnesia." We had to be taught to forget so we could learn to live together. But we don't seem to be able to stop forgetting. Remembering is dangerous; amnesia is dangerous, too. Dr. Woodside's concern is the damage done when our representatives abroad—he's thinking of Southeast Asia—blunder because of their lack of historical sensitivity. American amnesia is quite as destructive at home. The notion that 1776 was the "first libertarian revolution" (expressed by a minority party's presidential nominee)[1]

1. *The New York Times,* August 31, 1975.

is an example of amnesia. Here the notion of "liberty" is made to mean something never meant by the participants in the 1776 discussions. "Liberty" as an excuse for the willful hedonism which is dissolving our families and turning our cities into hells is a menace. Preachers in a thousand pulpits should labor in 1976 to restore the notion of liberty to its context of responsibility.[2]

Mexicans and Puerto Ricans excepted, America has finished assimilating. Despite their desperate invoking of Christendom's ancient enemy to fight assimilation and preserve ties to the African past, even Black Muslims are Americans at bottom. As pilgrims to the homeland in the Congo, Nigeria, or Tanzania know, what America does she does thoroughly. They return sadly, their wills resisting, their hearts indelibly American.

What mystery unites us? The white traveler at American Express discovers an identity he shares with his fellow, black, American tourist which he does not share with his own racial cousins on the street outside. In Sweden and Canada, fugitives from conscription know that love of country is deeper than approval of system.

It may be that to have assimilated the Germans, whose tough combination of national and religious loyalties still prove formidable obstacles for Rumanian or Brazilian unity, is the greatest demonstration of the power of the Americanization process. Whatever the case, we're all assimilated. At America's two hundredth birthday the Lutheran community, too, is totally unhyphenated, loyal—and forgetful.

Now that our primary problem is no longer to become one nation, it is safe to make a serious investigation of the past, in case there is something we have forgotten which may be of assistance in planning for the future. The old idea of the "American Melting Pot" is currently under attack. But there still exists a real obligation for each self-conscious minority to contribute to the commonweal whatever it can from its own experience.

2. One helpful book: Bernard Bailyn, *The Ideological Origins of the American Revolution* (Cambridge, Mass.: The Belknap Press of Harvard University Press, 1967).

I suggest that the Lutheran minority can enrich the discussion of the American Revolution and its Bicentennial significance by drawing certain inferences from its larger setting in the Reformation.

Apart from a few, distinguished exceptions, the participants in the Philadelphia discussions of 1776 were Protestants. Each of the major themes in that discussion, as listed by Dr. Bailyn in his *Ideological Origins*—the writings of the European Enlightenment, the English Common Law, the Covenant theology of Puritan New England—was profoundly influenced one way or another by the Reformation. Even their use of the ancient classical authors was determined by interests aroused, ultimately, by the Reformation. Involved in that century-long and thoroughly Protestant struggle for republican government in Britain and America, the Fathers of our country were interested only in the history which could explain the dynamics of the Roman republic.[3]

Three-quarters of the Lutheran immigrants who reached these shores abandoned their confession. There were a good many reasons to account for it. One of them was a perfectly reasonable question put to them by Protestant missionaries: now that you are in America, why don't you have an American religion? There still is a Lutheran community, committed with various degrees of enthusiasm to the Lutheran confessions. In a formal sense, since it is confessed by loyal Americans, the Lutheran faith can be said to be an American one. But the missionaries' question persists: the Lutheran consensus differs at significant points with the religious consensus which, consciously or unconsciously, shaped those discussions two hundred years ago. If, as I believe, it is precisely at the point of the religious presuppositions that some of the major problems of American history have developed, the Lutheran perspective can be valuable in any discussion which seeks to evaluate the American ideology.

3. Ibid., p. 25.

Lutheran Credibility

Before Lutherans dare raise their voices in the New World, they have the record of four hundred years to account for. What could possibly come from sixteenth century Saxony to challenge the brilliance of the political achievement of Anglo-Saxony? The Founding Fathers were not much impressed with the Lutheran political record. In fact, among the horrible examples of tyranny they wished to avoid in America, they mentioned specifically two Lutheran princes—their majesties of Sweden and Denmark —right along with the Turkish Pasha.[4] Nobody has been unkind enough to blame the Lutheran profession of the other Lutheran prince—George III—for his tyranny, about which the Declaration had unkind things to say. But there still is a wide dismay among political scientists, who suspect that the father of national socialism may have been Luther himself.[5] The suspicion, fanned during World War II into flame, still smolders. According to hundreds of university lecturers and, increasingly, Marxists, Luther was an uncreative reactionary, a downright counterrevolutionary. How, in the face of all this, can a Lutheran viewpoint be *credible,* especially if it has anything to do with politics?

And how about the Missouri Synod business?

Lutherans currently have a rather bad press; the newspaper accounts of the current crisis in the Lutheran Church–Missouri Synod certainly have a bad effect on the Lutheran *image.* But credibility is something else. The crisis of the Missouri Synod has little to do with our reflecting on American foundations from a specifically theological standpoint, because it has little to do with Lutheran theology, other than the question of internal church authority.

The detailed accounts of the deliberations of the synod show an angry majority, composed largely of laymen who are not theologically trained, in their impatience to work their will,

4. Ibid., p. 64.

5. E.g., William Montgomery McGovern, *From Luther to Hitler: The History of Fascist-Nazi Political Philosophy* (Cambridge, Mass.: Houghton-Mifflin, 1941).

sweeping theological discourse aside as irrelevant. They have an irreproachable *legal,* constitutional right to do so. The question is how that relates to the right to make doctrinal decisions. Two sacred traditions are in conflict: the Lutheran confessions, on the basis that authority is in the Word of God, assign the power of making decisions on questions of doctrine to the teaching office, that is, to those who have been *called,* and, presumably, trained. To put it as clearly as possible, the (less sacred!) conviction that power comes from the people is, in this case, in direct conflict with the confessions themselves. The difficulties of the Missouri Synod should set off a long-overdue discussion on the church's *magisterium*—the teaching office: does it inhere in a parliamentary majority?

But that is an internal ecclesiastical problem; it need detain us no longer.

Observe the Swedish and Danish tyrants. The fact that Sweden and Denmark have developed since 1776 into free and stable democracies without violence and without developing some of the flaws of American democracy suggests that left to itself (not the case in Germany!) Lutheran social ethics tend toward fostering healthy and equitable societies.[6]

How about the charges that Luther prepared the way for Hitler? First of all, most of them are based on the assumption, very flattering to Luther, but unfounded nonetheless, that the Reformer of Wittenberg was responsible for everything that took place after 1517. Even the Marxists, who are otherwise obstinate in insisting that history is not determined by personalities, but by vast economic movements, make an exception for Luther, in order to hold him *personally* responsible for the subsequent reactionary course of German politics.[7] Karl Barth, whose brilliance as an historian matched that of his systematic theology, should have avoided the sweeping generalization which identi-

6. One of George Forell's arguments in *Faith Active in Love* (New York: The American Press, 1954).

7. The Russian, Heinz Kamnitzer, for example, discussed by Abraham Friesen, *Reformation and Utopia: The Marxist Interpretation of the Reformation and Its Antecedents* (Wiesbaden: Franz Steiner Verlag, 1974), p. 186.

fied Luther's teaching exactly with that of his nineteenth and twentieth century followers.[8] The book most responsible for convincing Americans of the relationship of Luther and Hitler is William Shirer's *The Rise and Fall of the Third Reich*. This journalist says that "Luther's siding with the princes in the peasant uprising, which he had largely inspired, and his passion for political autocracy, ensured a mindless and provincial political absolutism which reduced the vast majority of the German people to a horrible torpor and a demeaning subservience."[9]

The theologian Hans Iwand has done a more careful investigation of the relationship between Reformation theology and the dismal history of German political science. A member of the generation who had to try to reconstruct things in Germany after the "zero-point" of the World War II defeat, he convinces the reader, I think, that he would have denounced St. Paul himself if he had found that he had contributed to the rise of Hitler!

He found that it was Philip Melanchthon, Luther's increasingly independent faculty colleague, who was responsible for the fatal mix of ideas which prepared the way for absolutism. Melanchthon mixed notions from Aristotle with Luther's separated church and state.

It was not Luther's prophetic visions, but Melanchthon's "simple, lucid and therefore so misleading" *textbooks* which determined what the next generation would think. His *Loci praecipui theologici* went through *two hundred and eight-six editions*! Iwand says that it was that textbook which "basically determined political science and social science in post-Reformation Germany."[10] Thus in a fashion subtle enough to have escaped battalions of historical generalizers, the Lutheran tradition was altered and falsified.

8. Cf. Karl Herz, "A Response to Hans Schwarz," *Lutheran Quarterly* 27, no. 1 (February 1975), pp. 76–79.
9. William Shirer, *The Rise and Fall of the Third Reich* (New York: Simon and Schuster, 1960), p. 91.
10. Hans Joachim Iwand, "Das Widerstandsrecht der Christen nach der Lehre der Reformatoren," in *Vorträge und Aufsätze*, ed. Dieter Schelling and Karl Gerhard Steck (Munich: Christian Kaiser Verlag, 1966), pp. 199–200.

Unlike Luther, Melanchthon was optimistic about man's nature and his capability of "virtue," as Aristotle was and as Cicero was. Since man was able to practice virtue, the obvious duty of the government was to cultivate it by practicing "discipline." It may be a bit too harsh to blame it *all* on Melanchton; there seems to have been a general will throughout Europe for states to practice ethical discipline. The French philosopher Michel Foucault observes, ". . . we see inscribed in the institutions of absolute monarchy—in the very ones that long remained the symbol of its arbitrary power—the great bourgeois, and soon republican, idea that virtue, too, is an affair of state, that decrees can be published to make it flourish, that an authority can be established to make sure it is respected."[11]

The church's task in all this was to reenforce the state. "Conscious of evil and of the Fall of the world, Christianity [according to Melanchthon] stands at the side of the state in the struggle against disrespect for authority."[12]

Melanchthon did not have a police state in mind; primarily an educator, he dreamed of a society which was benevolent, paternalistic.

> It is from one end to another something ideal; it serves a higher purpose. It does not rule to guarantee peace and bread to its subjects, but to raise them, to educate them. As state it has a cultural function, and specifically one which concerns the final goals of mankind. The image of man in his God-given ultimacy is what determines the nature of the political task of the state.[13]

But precisely in his vision of a utopian order, Melanchthon excluded the very freedoms claimed by the French Declaration of the Rights of Man or the American Declaration of Independence."[14]

Luther's political ethic, in contrast, "denies ultimacy, permanence and religious meaning to anything worldly but by that

11. Michel Foucault, *Madness and Civilization* (New York: Vintage Books edition, Random House, 1973), p. 61.

12. Iwand, "Das Widerstandsrecht der Christen," pp. 199–200.

13. Ibid.

14. Ibid., p. 205.

very denial liberates the secular order to be a truly human sphere, which man may enjoy and even love, so long as he does not make it an idol."[15]

The impossibility of understanding the period of the Reformation and its effect on our political institutions from a purely secular standpoint is never so clear as in the effect of Melanchthon's doctrine of sin on his fateful role as forerunner of political absolutism.

> Whoever overlooks the Fall of man can never recognize the reality of the world—which cannot be ruled without force. The order of political ethics is made for the fallen world, and does not have the task of redeeming it, but only to protect it from the final chaos, so that the church can carry on her work of redemption with proclamation directed to the individual.[16]

It is worth noticing that Barth and Engels and Shirer and others, in making judgment on Luther's political effect, always consider him as a national German figure and not as an ecumenical authority—which is how he is considered in Scandinavia at least. Melanchthon, *Praeceptor Germaniae*—teacher of Germany, to give him his most popular title, has had far less influence in the North. That the Northern countries, far more dominated by Luther's theology than his own homeland was, should have developed as they have, makes the problem of Luther's influence a good deal more complex than the generalizers think it to be!

In the next section, we shall show that the Lutheran Reformation in some ways is the ultimate source of crucial elements of the American tradition. The Lutheran tradition nevertheless has never had much direct effect on American institutions.

But it has never had full and direct effect on *any* political institutions. ". . . [the] radical implications of Luther's rediscovered biblical perspectives were never fully translated into social reality,"[17] not even in Scandinavia. At a time when Amer-

---

15. John M. Tonkin, "Luther's Interpretation of Secular Reality," *Journal of Religious History* VI, 2 (December 1970), p. 149.
16. Ibid.
17. Ibid.

icans are not so sure as they once were about the infallibility of their *"new order of the ages,"* Luther's biblical insights may have something to tell us.

THE REVOLUTION AND THE OTHER REVOLUTION

The Lutheran Revolution

Mr. Molotov was once invited, or at least there is a legend that says he was, to address a convocation of the Daughters of the American Revolution. He walked to the podium, took a long look at the orchidaceous and lorgnetted ladies before him, and with a wicked gleam in his eye began his speech with the greeting: "fellow revolutionaries!" But Mr. Molotov knew perfectly well that there was something different about his revolution.

The Bicentennial is being observed at a time when all Americans are conscious of having been bested in war by a committed Communist movement. It is also a time when the appeal *our* revolution once had in the world is being replaced by the attraction of *their* revolution. Consequently, one of the most important questions to discuss is the nature of revolution. We all know a good deal already about the difference between the revolts of 1776 and 1917. What the framework of the Protestant Reformation can do for us is to show us something about their basic nature at a very early stage of development.

We have it on the authority of Friedrich Engels himself that what we call the "Reformation" is really the "early bourgeois *revolution.*" It is a movement whose basic theme is economics, not religion, and its center is the revolt of the peasants in 1525 and 1526.[18] The "solidarity," as they put it, between the peasants' conviction and their own that in some mystical way their shared outrage was a source of political authority, is part of official Communist doctrine. They see, too, that there is no real

18. Friedrich Engels, *The German Revolutions: The Peasant War in Germany,* and *Germany: Revolution and Counter-Revolution.* (Chicago and London: University of Chicago Press, 1967), p. 19.

difference between the peasants' belief that they could construct Christ's kingdom on earth if their revolt worked and their own faith in the proletarian paradise. That Thomas Muentzer, the peasant leader, talked the language of Christian theology presents no problem to them, since Muentzer's authority was not scripture, but *his own inner conviction*.[19]

Engels, who really didn't know a great deal about the history of the sixteenth century, must be corrected. There were not one but *two* important political revolutions in the sixteenth century —both of them unsuccessful. They ended precisely twenty-five years apart. They are: 1526, the Peasants' revolution; 1551, the Lutheran revolution. Since no one I know, except for the Jesuits in the bad old days when "revolution" was a bad word, uses the term "Lutheran revolution," I had better explain it. ·

Luther was convinced that the real revolutionary force in history is biblical preaching. He knew, of course, what Theodore Roosevelt knew, and what we discussed in the last chapter, that rulers have to achieve political unity. Instinctively, all politicians know it. "They are the builders," he says. "They must see to it that their building has no crack, rent, or disfiguration." He was, typically, explaining the Bible—this time Psalm 118, verse 22: "The stone which the builders rejected has become the head of the corner." He goes on, in an explanation which leaves no room for calling his ideas on politics "static," to emphasize the future; Christ's kingdom would come in opposition to the efforts of those who labor for total human unity.[20]

Where Melanchthon encouraged theology students and law students to consider clergymen as assistants to the government, fostering unity and combating disobedience, Luther says that the preacher is a *rabble-rouser*. "He is a rabble-rouser who misleads the people whom they have so beautifully edified, ordered, and

19. On the Marxist interpretation of Muentzer see Abraham Friesen, *Reformation and Utopia: The Marxist Interpretation of the Reformation and Its Antecedents* (Wiesbaden: Franz Steiner Verlag, 1974), pp. 13 ff., *passim.*

20. "The Beautiful Confitemini," *Luther's Works,* American Edition [*AE*], vol. 14, p. 97.

organized. His way of doing things is entirely different from theirs."[21]

When Napoleon marched into Vienna and officially abolished the tottering remains of the Holy Roman Empire, hardly anyone noticed. The old order of the ages was already dead, and needed only the *coup de grâce*. The decisive *coup* had been Luther's, when in refusing to obey the imperial government in religious matters, he began unraveling the fabric of the old order. Since we take separation of church and state for granted these days, it takes a bit of strenuous remembering to understand how revolutionary his preaching was. "At a blow Christendom was resolved into a group, if not of states in the full sense, at least of territorial magistracies, independent and secular. The civil magistrate became at once the only guardian of law and order. . . ."[22]

We could just as well date the "new order of the ages" that the great American dollar bill advertises, at the moment that Luther dared tell his earthly lord that he could not do otherwise. Luther's effect on politics still hasn't been agreed on: ". . . the complex of questions concerning authority in the Lutheran area, in spite of enlightening studies on the doctrine of the Two Kingdoms as a theological basis, has not been studied well enough. A consensus on the facts about Luther's theoretical and practical position on authority and that of early Lutheranism has not yet emerged."[23]

One reason is that a long succession of German governments was afraid of sedition. The opinion of Ernst Troeltsch that the net political effect of the Reformation was two more centuries of the Middle Ages was, as John Tonkin says, a correct political judgment. But it is also true, as Professor Tonkin adds, that the "recognition of its truth should not blind us to the essentially revolutionary elements in Luther's thought. His achievement is not to be ignored because its potentialities were not fully rea-

21. Ibid.
22. F. J. C. Hearnshaw, *The Social and Political Ideas of Some Great Thinkers of the Renaissance and Reformation* (New York: Barnes and Noble, 1925, facsimile reprint, 1967), p. 174.
23. Heinz Scheible, *Das Widerstandsrecht als Problem der deutschen Protestanten 1523–1546* (Gütersloh: Gerd Mohn, 1969), p. 5.

lized in socio-political terms." There is, in fact, a dark suspicion that the full truth about the Lutheran discussion on the right to resist authority was *surpressed*.[24]

Think of the barons extracting the *Magna Carta* from a reluctant King John at Runnymede. Now project the picture to a larger, imperial, size. Now there are dukes dealing with the emperor Charles V. In Nuremberg in 1532 and in Frankfurt in 1539 they extracted from him the agreement that, in exchange for promises of military assistance, he would grant them freedom from religious laws, specifically by dropping charges against them in the Supreme Court—the *Reichskammergericht*. We're still at the point of the Reformation's fresh power. The princes were translating into the very center stage of world diplomacy Luther's biblical insight that Christ's kingdom "is not of this world" and cannot therefore be regulated by the princes of the world—the "builders."

Most Americans agree with the Baptist Roger Williams, who said the same thing—to his acute discomfort and ultimate banishment—in Massachusetts. The Puritan theology of the "covenant" had managed to restore that state of affairs in which state and church were mixed up again. It makes little difference how he came to that position[25]—the correction of the dangerous "covenant" ideas were overcome, and what Luther, what the princes of the League of Smalcald, fought for has become firm American tradition.

The situation in Germany was tense; such bargaining would not establish a lasting peace. The doctrine of the Two Kingdoms was nothing less than a challenge to the very structure of the thousand-year order of European society. In the tense atmosphere in which everyone expected war, the lawyers and theologians together hammered out the political doctrine which became—despite the later frustration of Luther's political in-

---

24. Ibid.

25. George Jellinek says that William's intellectual development is not yet fully explained. "Die Erklärung der Menschen- and Bürgerrechte," *Zur Geschichte der Erklärung der Menschenrechte,* ed. Roman Schnur (Darmstadt: Wissenschaftliche Buchgesellschaft, 1974), p. 44.

fluence—the effective legacy of the Smalcaldic League of princes to the long Protestant struggle for republican government—"the doctrine of the Lesser Magistrates."[26]

That doctrine can be stated most elegantly from a theological standpoint. It was essentially a radically new way of looking at Rom. 13:1–2, the passage which in the Middle Ages had been a major inhibition to those who suffered from tyranny: "Let every person be subject to the governing authorities. For there is no authority except from God, and those that exist have been instituted by God. Therefore he who resists the authorities resists what God has appointed, and those who resist will incur judgment." Melanchthon understood by "instituted by God" what Aristotle understood—a kind of divinization of the status quo.

But it was primarily the *laymen* in the conversations—the attorneys—who convinced Luther and the other theologians that they ought to be willing to be consistent with their own Two Kingdom theology and let the secular government *be* secular. The result was that the dukes, who knew that long ago *their* votes had, in fact, created the emperor, got away with the argument that that also made *them* "governing authorities,"—in the sense of Romans 13! And, so their argument went, if that was so, they could "bear the sword" (Rom. 13:4) *even against the emperor,* if he became a tyrant.

Their understanding of "tyranny" was the violation of the principle of separation of church and state by attempting to enforce the medieval faith. Although historians of law have thought sometimes that ideas of natural rights or the social contract were the most important elements in the rise of democracy, at least the legal scholar Kurt Wolzendorff says that this idea, the doctrine of the lesser Magistrates, was the crucial one which began the modern development of democratic theory.[27]

26. Cf. Richard Roy Benert. "Inferior Magistrates in Sixteenth Century Political and Legal Thought." Ph.D. dissertation, St. Paul, University of Minnesota, 1967.

27. Kurt Wolzendorff, *Staatrecht und Naturrecht in der Lehre vom Widerstandsrecht des Volkes gegen richtwidrige Ausübung der Staatsge-*

For when the Germans wanted to have no more to do with that doctrine, the French Huguenots discovered, to their relief, from the Lutherans, that their king's *ministers* and the *officers* of the kingdom, too, had that authority which St. Paul said comes from God.

To read a history of Latin America is to confront centuries of suffering caused, at bottom, by the ferocity of the Counter-Reformation's resistance to the doctrine of the Two Kingdoms and consequently of the secularity of government, which was the theoretical basis of the doctrine of the Lesser Magistrates. The same crown of Spain, which was the soul of the resistance to Luther, was the only source of legitimacy for a vast territory which still stretches from our own borders to near the South Pole.

Luther's insight into Romans 13 meant ultimately that whereas God wills that government exist, he has not specified *which* government. Neither Luther nor Calvin ever approved sedition; no *private* person could resist authority. But authority was not concentrated in the *crown*; the rays of the crown, indeed, are meant to be the rays of the sun, and betray a mystical Germanic and Oriental identification of the government and God!

At their revolution, the countries of Latin America repudiated the Spanish crown. And at the same time—ominously—they lost the precious sense of *legitimacy*;[28] they became at the mercy of cynical *caudillos,* in a series of essentially meaningless revolutions. The current discussion in Latin America on "liberation theology" correctly sees a way out of the morass on the basis of Christian leadership. Before the "liberation theologians" incorporate too much of Marxism, however, they should examine the revolutionary ideas inherent in the Christian tradition itself and flickeringly apparent in the Reformation. The considerable

walt (Breslau: M. & H. Marcus, 1916; reprinted, Aalen: Scientia Verlag, 1961), p. 12. By "modern development of democratic theory," I mean that discussion which begins with the French Huguenot wars.

28. Stephen Clissold, *Latin America: A Cultural Outline* (New York: Harper and Row, Colophon Books, 1965), p. 12.

Lutheran population in South America, too, should stir itself to discover its own revolutionary tradition.

Luther was defeated politically, but not without one spectacular last act. Like other politicians, the princes were flexible and they recognized the political realities of having lost their war for the Lutheran cause. Without a trace of embarrassment the princes, who had fought for the separation of church and state, went about transforming their churches into departments of their own governments. That, after all, is what all German princes had lusted to do since the first missionaries appeared in the misty German forests. Melanchthon's approval was quite convenient.

There was a last pocket of military resistance—the city of Magdeburg. It offered religious freedom for the pastors and theologians whose convictions were less flexible than those of the princes. Magdeburg offered, in addition, freedom of the press, at a time when press censorship was being invented. The Lutheran theological community there proceeded to prove—for the first time, it seems—the power of what the Communists now call *agitprop* through the torrent of publications, directed against the imperial government—and Philip Melanchthon.

In one of their publications, the *Confession, Instruction and Warning,* they have left a classical formulation of the doctrine of the Lesser Magistrates:

> When high authority unjustly presumes to persecute with force not only the persons of those subject to its rule, but also their divine or natural rights; and when it suspends and destroys true doctrine and worship, the lesser magistrate is under divine obligation to defend itself and those subject to it as best it can against that authority.[29]

John Calvin, be it noted, never went so far as this Lutheran justification of armed resistance. The very earliest American government was able to pass laws against sedition, and with no sense of hypocrisy—ultimately because there was a well-

29. Quoted in Oliver K. Olson, "Theology of Revolution," *Sixteenth Century Journal,* vol. 3, no. 1 (April 1972), p. 71.

established Protestant tradition of the *right* of subordinate authorities to exercise legitimate, God-given authority.

There is a rising interest in this history among Marxists. It is therefore imperative that we make a strenuous effort to overcome our amnesia about our own tradition. In spite of those imperious "Lutheran" princes who swept the Magdeburg incident, well-known as a symbol of resistance in the sixteenth century,[30] into the historical dustbin, we must develop the implications of the Magdeburg resistance. It is a representative of the Communist-sponsored Yugoslav Academy, Miro Mircovic, who testifies that the democracy implicit in their use of the Lesser Magistrate doctrine—"lesser magistrates" for them were not only city governments, but, in strict Lutheran fashion, also fathers of families!—was matched by a concern for the common people, which he contrasts with Melanchthon's "feudalism."[31]

The twenty percent of the students at the Lutheran theological faculty of Göttingen who voted Communist in the 1974 university elections are matched by American students horrified by the evils in our system. The Lutheran revolution, which was more than "spiritual," but took on, in 1550 and 1551 in Magdeburg, quite realistic political form, suggests that achieving equality and fighting tyranny in society are also possible in the name of God's law. Lutheran congregations, in their constitutions, have demonstrated their doctrinal "solidarity" with the Magdeburg resistance to Melanchthon's alterations by insisting on the *unaltered* Augsburg Confession (the Formula of Concord's positions are largely those of Magdeburg rather than of Melanchthon's Wittenberg). They should now also consider political solidarity!

Forgetting that the Lutheran confession led straight to Magdeburg made it possible for Marx to make a plausible claim that

30. Cynthia Grant Schoenberger, "The Confession of Magdeburg and the Lutheran Doctrine of Resistance." Ph.D. dissertation, Columbia University, 1972, p. 110.
31. Miro Mircovic, *Matija Vlacic Ilirik* (Zagreb: Yugoslavian Academy, 1960), *passim*.

the Lutheran faith—which is primarily what he had in mind—was the "opium of the people." Consider what might have happened.

The Proto-Communist Revolution

In university classrooms and Marxist meetings all over the United States and Europe, students are being horrified these days with Luther's reaction to the peasant revolt: "Therefore let everyone who can, smite, slay, and stab, secretly or openly, remembering that nothing can be more poisonous, hurtful or devilish than a rebel. It is just as when one must kill a mad dog; if you do not strike him, he will strike you, and the whole land with you."[32]

What should the pastor do, should a student confront him with these words at Christmas vacation? Are they bad taste, perhaps, to be balanced with all the great inspiration we owe to the Reformer? Unconvincing—in fact, they come from the center of his theology. Luther knew that if the peasants won their revolt, they would build a society in which law would be based on their own collective outrage or, to put it in Communist terms, on *class ideology*.

The suffering incurred by the peasants in their defeat at Frankenhausen in 1525 was bloody and tragic; but it was nothing like the unspeakable agonies in that land where class ideology, in fact, has become the source of the law—*The Gulag Archipelago*. In one passage, Aleksandr Solzhenitsyn evokes the terror of a Russian trial. All the ritual of the law is played out, but behind the courtroom stage-set, through a curtain. Once in a while the flicker of a pipe being lit betrays One whose *will* determines the law. Group dynamics being what they are, the definition of law as class ideology must be concentrated in the will of one or a few.

And where the law is not high, outside the community's consensus, there is no appeal. Ghandi's "march to the sea" de-

32. Martin Luther, "Against the Robbing and Murdering Hordes of Peasants," *Luther's Works, AE,* vol. 46, pp. 54–55.

pended for its political effect, ultimately, on Christian preaching through the centuries. This had left a conviction that just law, somehow, may not be exactly the same as the will of the people in power. But the demonstrations of the "Hungarian Spring" had no similar effect on Russia where by definition the will of the party is identical with the law.

The enormity of altering the very basis of justice on earth dwarfs all secondary considerations—even the legitimate grievances of the peasants! At what point in Russian history did the possibility of an appeal against the injustice of those in power disappear? Solzhenitsyn says that it was the point at which the young people, revolted by the evils of the Czarist government, began to consider going to prison as something honorable, or when army officers began to refuse to shake the hand of a policeman. "And the more the prison system weakened, the more clearly evident were the triumphant ethics of the political prisoners, and the more visibly did the members of the revolutionary parties realize their strength and regard their own laws as superior to those of the state."[33]

What Solzhenitsyn has isolated in agonizing retrospect, Luther recognized very early, urging that it be nipped in the bud. In "Against the Heavenly Prophets in the Matter of Images and Sacraments,"[34] Luther puts his finger on the jugular vein: "Due to great fulness of the spirit they forget civil discipline and manners, and no longer fear and respect anyone but themselves alone" (p. 101). The question was not whether the statues in the churches which the mobs were smashing should be destroyed or not; the question was where the smashing-authority had come from.

There are certain events in history whose significance escapes all except those who are willing to wrestle with ultimate questions. The excuse offered by Robert Crossley in his *Luther and the Peasants' War,* in speculating on whether Luther acted as he did because he was by now relatively well-to-do, is unaccept-

33. Aleksandr Solzhenitsyn, *The Gulag Archipelago* (New York: Harper and Row, 1973), pp. 458–459.
34. *Luther's Works, AE,* vol. 40, pp. 73 ff.

able: "the secular historian will overlook much that interests the theologian."[35] One might as well write a book about Henry Ford without mentioning the automobile!

The two revolutions of the sixteenth century cannot be forced into the superficial categories of "conservative" and "liberal" or "counterrevolutionary" and "proletarian." If we *remember* carefully enough and get our history straight, Luther is concerned not about the differentiation of classes among men. Anyone who has observed, with George Orwell, that in Communist societies some people are "more equal" than others, will agree that a Marxist revolution does little to solve that problem. Luther is concerned with nothing less than preaching that all authority comes from God alone.[36] It comes through *external* revelation.

From a certain point of view, the Lutheran Reformation is "magisterial" and that represented by the peasants' revolt is "radical." But that point of view is superficial in comparison to the underlying problem. Friesen sees the confrontation between Luther and the peasants' insurrection as a struggle between those of (1) the Augustinian tradition, who see a basic conflict between God and evil, and who also show a consequent willingness to live with deep ambiguities in society; and those of (2) the tradition stemming from the monk Joachim of Fiore, of Thomas Muentzer, Hegel and Marx, who mystically identify authority with man's collective will and who also expect that historical struggle will bring an earthly paradise.

It is on that level, not the level of "conservative" and "liberal," that the two revolutions of the sixteenth century must be judged. Luther did not side with one class against another. His question was: where does the law come from?

---

35. Robert Crossley, *Luther and the Peasants' War* (New York: Exposition Press, 1974), p. vii.
36. This raises questions about whether it is significant in Christian-Communist dialogues if the Communist party accepts religious members or not. The important matter is not whether one is "religious" or not; the crucial consideration is whether authority comes from the party or from *outside* the party, or to put it in another way, whether the Two Kingdoms are kept distinct!

WHERE THE LAW COMES FROM

Civil Religion

What makes those people in Washington think they can run our lives for us? What *right* do they have? They aren't saying. And their argument that they are too busy passing the laws to philosophize about them is not convincing. The debate on the question was fitful and unfocused in 1776 and it is now, but the question should not be ignored—*who gives them the right?*

In considering the American Revolution as part of the larger context of the Reformation, we have noticed that at the beginning of the "new order" two answers were given. According to the movement Marx and Engels recognize as proto-Communist, laws must be based ultimately on the consensus of conscience of the class in society which had been ill used; according to what we have chosen to call the "Lutheran revolution" because of its specifically political effects, especially its focus in the Magdeburg resistance movement, authority is external and derives from God.

The brilliance of the conversations of 1776 and of the political structures which resulted from them is unparalleled, but their treatment of the provenance of the law represents no advance over the sixteenth century. Both points of view are still present, but now woven so closely together in a fabric that the individual threads of thought are difficult to isolate.

Some statements give the impression that authority resides in man himself—in us, the people. The wild, disreputable ones who raise ceremonial fists these days at assemblies of the outraged had their counterparts in colonial America in the civilized, reputable people who wrote the Massachusetts Bill of Rights. They all agree that our country not only should assign "power to the people"—they also insist that power *comes from the people,* something that Abraham Lincoln would not say. By the time they wrote the Massachusetts document the ill-conceived theological construct called "covenant theology" or "federal theology" had undergone an inevitable secularizing process. What remained was a naked social contract: "The body-politic is

21

formed by a voluntary association of individuals; it is a social compact by which the whole people covenants with each citizen and each citizen with the whole people that all shall be governed by certain laws for the common good."[37]

On the other side are the garbage men and Martin Luther King, who could have carried that old revolutionary flag with the slogan, "an appeal to heaven." Laws which varied too much from God's justice, they meant to say, were no laws at all. Requiring certain people to sit in humiliation in the back of the bus is *unjust,* even if it is backed by the law books and a majority.

The Declaration of Independence not only is a protest against the tyranny of a remote king. It takes the side of Martin Luther King's appeal to the higher law of God. Its assertion of "inalienable rights" is a stinging rebuke to the dangerous Massachusetts notion of "covenant"; law is not created by human decision, but by the will of the Creator. The threat to freedom inherent in the Massachusetts document was seen very clearly in Virginia, whose Bill of Rights reads quite differently: "That all men are by nature equally free and have certain inherent rights, of which, when they enter into a state of society, they cannot *by any compact* deprive or divest their posterity."[38]

Walter Lippmann once said that "our civilization can be maintained and restored only by remembering and rediscovering the truths, and by re-establishing the habits on which it was founded."[39] Good advice. American amnesia affects us like a kind of insanity. But when we remember the past with enough strenuous effort, we find no settled answers. The question about the authority of the law is not settled by the American Constitution, nor by the consensus of the sixteenth century. It was unclear in the great law code itself, of Justinian, which summed up the legal wisdom of the Romans.[40] At bottom, there is no satis-

37. Quoted by Jellinek, "Erklärung der Menschen- und Bürgerrechte," p. 21.
38. Ibid., p. 21.
39. Quoted by James Reston, "The Forgotten Civilities," *The New York Times,* September 5, 1975.
40. Edward S. Corwin, "The 'Higher Law' Background of American Constitutional Law," *Harvard Law Review* 42 (1928–30). Reprinted (Ithaca, New York: Cornell University Press, 1955), p. 4.

fying basis on which we can build the judicial and legislative systems. The documents of the American government are based on a masterful mix of the two presuppositions. But in the end we still are faced with the shattering prophetic command: "choose!"

It was not a theologian, but an historian, Perry Miller, who made clear the importance of the "covenant" concept for the development of American civilization. His works, which constitute "the most significant work of research in the history of ideas in America,"[41] *describe* the federal (covenant) theology to an amnesiac public. The Lutheran tradition, which has been highly aware of its opposition to the "covenant" notion for four hundred years, now that it is a fully assimilated *American* tradition, should go beyond Miller and *criticize* the tradition theologically.

It is a matter of some importance that recent studies in the Old Testament show that the Pilgrim Fathers' reading of the Old Testament was inaccurate. The "covenant" arrangement in Israel, which constituted the model, was not reciprocal, somehow, as they thought, but completely *one-sided.*[42] Their emphasis on the importance of man's assent to the law is the continuation of a theme already noticeable in the Middle Ages;[43] and to a large extent due to the emphasis on human assent in the philosophical movement known as nominalism. Luther emphasized the terms, "Old Testament" and "New Testament," which are expressions of grace alone, rather than the word, *"Bund,"* or "Covenant," as is clear in the brilliant article by Dr. Kenneth Hagen of Marquette University.[44]

It is worth noting that the immediate source for the presence

41. Ursula Brumm, *Puritanismus und Literatur in Amerika* (Darmstadt: Wissenschaftliche Buchgesellschaft, 1973), p. 11.

42. Cf. George Mendenhall, "Law and Covenant in Israel and the Ancient Near East," *The Biblical Archaeologist* 17, no. 2 (May 1954), pp. 26–46 and no. 3 (September 1954), pp. 49–76.

43. Martin Geschat, "Bundnistheologie im Spätmittelalter," *Zeitschrift für Kirchengeschichte* 81 (1970), pp. 44–63.

44. Kenneth Hagen, "From Testament to Covenant in the Early Sixteenth Century," *The Sixteenth Century Journal,* vol. 3, no. 1 (April 1972), pp. 1–24.

of the "covenant" tradition among the Pilgrim Fathers is that very Thomas Muentzer with whom Marx and Engels find themselves in "solidarity." Muentzer's main activity was organizing the peasants in "covenants."

The Marxist historian, Max Steinmetz, worked out a way that Muentzer could be a Communist hero despite his being a theologian. Precisely that religious element, being concerned about God, watered down his revolutionary impact; but shorn of the religious trappings he "anticipated an idea for which neither the masses nor the historical dialectic had been ready. . . ."[45]

What happened in the course of the inevitable legal agonies in colonial Massachusetts was that the "covenant" was shorn of its religious trappings. The second generation, unable to duplicate its fathers' religious experience and therefore unsure in large part of its being "saved," would have been excluded from civil rights, had the community followed the inexorable logic. Instead, they abandoned their theological convictions for practicality and conceived a "half-way covenant." By the time of the Massachusetts Bill of Rights, the religious trappings were gone and, for the first time in history, the "social contract" which was a beloved theme of European theorists was built into the hard reality of life, as a basis for the decisions of policemen and judges.

In a book called *Defining America,* Robert Benne and Philip Hefner propose that the United States return to the covenant theology, although, as they observe, the covenant "did not promote a caring relationship for the land, the poor, or the American and the black populations."[46] *Of course* it didn't. Civil rights belonged only to those who assented to the "covenant." Benne and Hefner, whose discussion tends to think primarily in terms of "symbols" in the manner of literary criticism or the theology of Paul Tillich, miss the important jurisprudential aspect of the "covenant" tradition—*it was translated into tyrannical law.*

45. Friesen, *Reformation and Utopia,* p. 215.
46. Robert Benne and Philip Hefner, *Defining America: A Christian Critique of the American Dream* (Philadelphia: Fortress Press, 1974), p. 110.

If they think by considering the covenant merely a "symbol" that "the hope of the American future is dependent, in this continuing Puritan tradition, upon the promise we as Americans make to the principles of a just and orderly internal life,"[47] they are saying something relatively harmless, although the "continuing Puritan tradition" is almost certainly responsible for the preposterous problem of the loyalty-oaths.

Of course the "Amerindian" was despised. A thousand sermons made the "parallels" clear. The Puritans were the covenant people. Old Europe was Egypt, the Atlantic Ocean the Jordan river, and America New Canaan. Even if they never actually had said it, what could prevent the New England Elect from seeing the American Indians as Canaanites? The shameful record of the American nation in its dealings with the Indians is due not to the Christian tradition, but partly to the inaccurate interpretation of it.

The false premise that nothing particularly *new* occurred when Jesus announced and inaugurated a New Testament (Covenant), but that it was another state in the history of the same old covenant of Moses, led inexorably, apart from the legal checks from an older tradition, to a reestablishment of a Jewish theocracy in the Massachusetts wilderness.

"The theocratic ideal, according to which the religious community, the Jewish 'Congregation' [precursor of the Christian 'Ecclesia'] coincided with the State . . . is expressly rejected by Christianity as satanic, [as] we need only recall [in] the temptation stories in the Gospels."[48]

Inevitably stripped of its religious foundation, the secular remainder was a proof of Rousseau's observation that a "social contract delivers over all rights to society."[49]

It was against that ominous tradition from Massachusetts that

---

47. Ibid., p. 25.
48. Oscar Cullmann. *The State in the New Testament* (New York: Charles Scribner's Sons, 1956), pp. 8–9.
49. Jellinek, "Erklärung der Menschen- und Burgerrechte," p. 5. He quotes Rousseau: "Ces clauses . . . se réduisant à une seule: savoir l'aliénation totale de chaque associé avec tous ses droits à toute la communauté." *Du contrat social* I, b.

the American Independence Declaration and the Bill of Rights were aimed. "The principles of the social contract . . . are hostile to any declaration of rights. What proceeds from them is not the right of the individual but the omnipotence of the legally limitless will of the community."[50] We should not be confused about the ominous nature of the idea by its association with the undeniable piety of New England. Nor should we overlook the historical circumstance that the theological mistakes of Massachusetts were corrected, not by the secular tradition of General Lafayette, as is often supposed, but by the theological tradition of Roger Williams, who, like Luther, demanded the institutional separation of church and state.[51]

What Williams fought for was built into the Bill of Rights, which drew a sharp boundary between the state and the individual. "The individual, consequently, is the subject of law not primarily through the state, but through his nature; he had unalienable, untouchable rights."[52]

Although the American intolerance of precision in religious discussion often makes the struggle of the two bases of legal authority obscure, it should now be clear to us that the same controversy over the root of the law's authority which we saw at the time of the Reformation is going on in a more subtle fashion at the founding of our nation. It should also be clear that here the Lutheran tradition fully agrees with the liberal tradition in America, in which Roger Williams stands out as a prophet.

The full implications of ascribing the *source* of power "to the people," revealed by banishments and executions of those in Massachusetts who did not *assent,* and by the agonies of Russian dissenters in the *Gulag,* do not in any way cast the idea of democracy in doubt. We have seen in the Magdeburg resistance episode that further extension of the authority "instituted by God," which Luther recognized could be extended to all Roman electors if *their* constitution wanted it that way. In Magdeburg not only the municipal government but also fathers of families

50. Ibid., p. 33.
51. Ibid., p. 54.
52. Ibid., p. 33.

were considered "instituted by God" and entitled to resist the emperor. The difference between the theological point of view, which sees authority vested in God alone, and the view which sees it as inherent in humanity is not that one is fascistic and the other democratic! They are *equally* "democratic," but not equally free!

The American Constitution has extended the franchise, whose development we can follow already in the sequence of the discussion from the Saxon court to the Magdeburg city hall, to nigh universality. The source of authority in the American tradition is ambiguous, but it is possible for Christians to argue that the power in democracy is God's power, entrusted to those called to the office of "elector."

A Nation under God

A great many leaders and philosophers have had deep misgivings about the wisdom of permitting the Christian church to exist in a society. And they had good reasons to wonder. To the extent that Christian preaching actually does what it is intended to do, it does create tensions. It complicates "the quest for the myths and images that pull the nation's life together in a meaningful whole," to use Benne and Hefner's description of the patriotic "civil religion."[53]

But if there is nothing beyond a "meaningful whole" in a state, there is tyranny. Caesar Augustus created a "meaningful whole" by inventing his interdenominational religion; the *Gulag Archipelago* discusses the difficulties inherent in a "meaningful whole." Even colonial Massachusetts had the making of a tyrannical "whole" until Christian good sense broke the bounds of the narrow theology which enslaved it.

Our survey has shown how American freedom owes largely to the intrusion of an absolute, an *apodictic,* law which is from outside the community. The Declaration of Independence and the Bill of Rights guarantee freedom precisely because they protect us from the notion that our law derives from the will of the majority.

53. Benne and Hefner, *Defining America,* p. 95.

That eliminating the preaching of the law can have frightful results is the theme of a *New York Magazine article,* which showed the influence on Richard Nixon of Norman Vincent Peale. "Above all," said James Conaway, "if you are thinking about Peale as a key to the Nixon mystery, note that the concept of repentance is conspicuously lacking in normanvincent-pealeism. Since the ideas of sin and repentance are essentially 'negative' they have no place in positive thinking, where self-reflection is replaced by remorseless persistence."[54]

The tendency to equate moral standards with popular consensus needs no documentation. With the idea that morals come simply from what the people want them to be, backed by the ominous power of the mass media to stir up lust and selfishness, our future is chaos, unless there is something to counteract it.

Perhaps this is the time for churches to take those flags out of their chancels as disillusioned German Lutherans also did when it dawned on them that their national will was not God's. Whatever we do, we must take steps to proclaim that legal authority ultimately comes from God.

A good deal of the blame, ironically, rests with the church, whose presence in society always divides loyalties and prevents society from being "whole." The long history of Christian resistance against kings who claimed divinity is totally responsible for the *secularity* of the "new order" of the United States. And ultimately the church is responsible for the ambiguity of Supreme Court decisions, which never come out and say where the law comes from.

The landmark case, *Reynolds v. United States,* for example, said that "the Mormons can believe anything they want, but engaging in marriage constitutes action and as such is subject to restriction by the state *to conform with the moral standards of the community.*"[55] It is an ambiguous decision. It stays with the limits set on the state by that determined, millennium-long

---

54. James Conaway, "God, Nixon, and Norman Vincent Peale," *New York Magazine* vol. 7, no. 29 (May 20, 1974), p. 50.

55. Leo Pfeffer, *God, Caesar and the Constitution: The Court as Referee of Church-State Confrontation* (Boston: Beacon Press, 1975), p. 31.

Christian campaign. But it can also be understood to say that power inheres in people.

It is the church which is responsible, too, for that confusion we have in dealing with communism. What do we *as a nation* hold up as an alternative to communism? Capitalism? Democracy? A higher standard of living? Nothing we counterpose to it as a nation will do, because our nation is not a "whole." And the presence of the church guarantees that it will never be— until the End.

Because the church has prevented the nation from being a whole, it is a tragedy that in large parts of the church Christians have lost interest in the law and the sources of its authority and have become almost totally absorbed in the individual and his or her religious experience. It would be a healthy development if the Bicentennial discussion stimulated us to think long and hard about the law.

There was a time when the idolatry of the human race expressed itself in adoring its own communal, mystical *representative,* the emperor. But the church was not confused. Rather than admit the emperor was a god, Christians died. Blundering through the long Middle Ages, the church was still always dimly aware that Christ's kingdom was not the same as Caesar's. The title of the popes, "vicar of Christ," is significant not so much because it was given to the popes, as it was taken away from the emperors, in a battle long ago for the doctrine of the Two Kingdoms.

Now that the church has dealt successfully with those kings who confused themselves with God, it finds itself confronted with a confusion between God and the people. That confusion is taking place both in the churches, where the sacred notion of a majority vote is replacing the thundering determination of the Reformation that teaching should be by those who are *called,* and in the state, even though "the attribution of supremacy to the Constitution on the ground solely of its rootage in popular will represents . . . a comparatively late outgrowth of American constitutional theory."[56]

56. See above, note 40.

The serpent in the garden suggested the enchanting possibility that man could be god. Despite the Christian influence at the formation of our country, which insisted that the law comes from God, our country is drifting into a dream of a society in which its own will is the highest law. Such a realization should be a signal for Christians to get back to the barricades and fight for what Christians have fought for in every generation.

It is difficult to answer the academics who remember the arrogance and clericalism of Massachusetts. It is difficult to answer the social reformers who equate judges and police with fascism. It is difficult to deal with church committees who see "authoritarian personalities" whenever a prophet appears. It is difficult to live down the memories of the inquisition or an absolutism consecrated by the church. And it is difficult for Americans, brought up to submit to majorities, to understand that authority comes from the Word of God.

The message that God is on the throne created the fruitful tension basic to Western society, caused the Reformation of the church, guaranteed our own liberties in the Bill of Rights, and holds back the tidal wave of social evils. This message comes from no other source than from the church. In our country's third century it is our turn to say it.

Clarence L. Lee

Church and State
in Tension

CHURCH AND STATE IN CONFUSION

Almost overlooked by Americans as they observe the two hundredth birthday of their country is the fact that the year 1976 marks a significant anniversary of another memorable event. In A.D. 476—exactly fifteen hundred years ago—the puppet emperor Romulus Augustulus was deposed by the Germanic mercenaries who, for all practical purposes, controlled the western part of the Roman Empire at that time. Regardless of the real significance of this event, the deposition of Romulus Augustulus has traditionally been adopted by historians as a convenient symbol for the "fall" of the Roman Empire. Like a day in July 1776, a day in August 476 was destined to be singled out as one of the so-called turning points of history that dramatically altered the course of human affairs and had far-reaching, almost incalculable social and political consequences.

It would be interesting and instructive to pursue the remarkable coincidence of these two significant anniversaries in the year 1976. Americans have always been fascinated by the parallels, real or unreal, between their own national experience and the experience of the Roman Empire. In recent years, this fascination has noticeably increased as more and more Americans, disturbed by what seemed to be an endless series of foreign and domestic crises, have found themselves wondering whether American civilization may not be caught up in the same pattern of decline which preceded Rome's fall.

31

The intensity with which parallels between the fortunes of Rome and the fortunes of America have been sought during the past ten years suggests that 1976, with its dual commemorative significance, would provide an ideal occasion for serious reflection on this matter. As America seeks to assess its strengths and weaknesses as a nation during its Bicentennial, it might do well to conduct that assessment, in part, at least, in the light of the landmark event with which it shares anniversary honors in 1976.

The present study, however, does not have such an assessment as its immediate concern. Our assignment in these three chapters is to analyze and interpret the relationship between church and state in the pre-Reformation period, an assignment that has its own compelling reason for calling attention to the event which has come to symbolize the fall of the Roman Empire. This event, as we hope to demonstrate in succeeding pages, was a major factor in shaping the basic pattern of church-state relations throughout much of the pre-Reformation period. Indeed, the distinctive character and direction which these relations assumed can be brought into sharp focus only by viewing them against the background of the developments and consequences typified by this event.

Thus, it is as an important and meaningful key to the fulfillment of our specific assignment that we have invoked an incident which also happens to have impressive commemorative associations at this particular time. Although these associations are not responsible for the fact that we have chosen the fall of Rome and what it signified as the point of departure for our investigation, they are nevertheless inescapable and can only enhance our discussion of church-state relations within the context of this truly remarkable year.

Church and State during the Middle Ages

When historians speak of church-state relations during the Middle Ages, they invariably find themselves resorting to words like "problem" or "struggle" or "contest" to describe the nature of those relations. This experience simply confirms the fact that a confrontation with the element of tension is inevitable in any investigation of the relationship between the two institutions during this particular period of history. Sometimes the tension lay beneath the surface and can be discerned and appreciated only by the specialist who is trained to look for such things. At other times, the tension betrayed itself so openly that no one can possibly fail to detect its presence. Whether subtle or overt, however, tension between church and state was a prominent and recurring motif in the medieval experience. It is not, indeed, too great an oversimplification to say that this motif constituted one of the most unyielding facts of life throughout the entire period.

There were, of course, many factors which contributed to this tension, some of them unique to the particular historical situations in which the affairs of church and state were actually contested. Still, there is one factor that has special importance and special interpretive value in our study. The very climate of tension—the unresolved contradiction running throughout church-state relations in the Middle Ages—can be traced back, in large part, to a complex of conditions and circumstances which we have chosen to call by its traditional title: the fall of the Roman Empire.

In the present context, the significance of Rome's fall (which was really, as we have already hinted, a series of developments signifying the erosion of imperial Rome's influence and control in the West, and only typified by the deposition of Romulus Augustulus in A.D. 476) was its immediate legacy of political instability and administrative weakness. This permitted the western church to assume a posture of independence vis-à-vis the state, a posture which in many respects came to suggest a kind of rivalry with the state.

In a very real way, the breakdown of effective political leadership in the West contained the seeds of a tradition which was to become a cherished part of the American way of life, the tradition, namely, which freed the church from control by the political establishment. At the same time, however, in terms of the medieval development itself, the church's exploitation of this breakdown for what often appeared to be its own political advantage contained the seeds of future strife between church and state.

The church confused its boundaries with those of the state—which is, in effect, what happened when it extended its sphere of influence so as to include many of the functions and prerogatives proper to the state. The church thereby opened itself to the constant threat of having its own proper sphere of influence exploited and compromised once the authority of the state was able to reassert itself. Far from accepting the secular prerogatives which the church had been able to assume in the absence of strong political leadership, the gradually revitalized states of western Europe were frequently tempted to challenge even the church's claims to autonomy in the realm of the sacred. Thus, if the church profited greatly from the political vacuum which existed at the beginning of its medieval development, it also suffered greatly because of that vacuum and the legacy of tension which it bequeathed to church-state relations throughout the Middle Ages.

The Byzantine Experience

In order to appreciate the significance of tension as an enduring dynamic in church-state relations in the West, it is useful—even essential—to contrast those relations with the situation that prevailed in the eastern or so-called Byzantine Empire. The very fact that this part of the Roman Empire did not experience a "fall" (until much later) was extremely important for the relationship between church and state in the East. Instead of being faced with a breakdown of the political order which the church could exploit, as it did in the West, the eastern church found itself within a state which was characterized by a continuity of political authority. A part of this continuity was the state's peculiar alliance with the church, an alliance which was important in and of itself, but which has added importance as a point of comparison for the pattern of church-state relations which developed in the West.

Although it is much too facile to sum up the entire relationship between church and state in the Byzantine Empire by the overworked term "caesaropapism," it is true that the right of the state, in the person of the caesar or emperor, to exercise influence in the affairs of the church was taken for granted in Byzantium in a way that would have been unthinkable in the West. "Caesaropapism" becomes a misnomer, however, when we observe that this exercise of influence worked both ways. It was also taken for granted in Byzantine society that the interests of the church were identical in every respect to those of the state and therefore could be used to shape and monitor the policies and programs of the state. For every case in which we find a Byzantine emperor "interfering" in the inner life of the church—including even the church's definition of its doctrine—we must remember the church's continual "interference" in the affairs of the state through its insistence on the "most Christian orthodoxy" not only of the emperor himself, but of all his dealings and subjects as well. If the state and its concerns were permanently mirrored in the Byzantine church, it is equally true that the church and its concerns were permanently mirrored in the Byzantine state.

What we are really dealing with in Byzantine society is a classic case of the confusion of the spheres of influence and interest proper to church and state, or, to use a more Lutheran expression, a confusion of the two kingdoms. By making the boundaries of church and state virtually coextensive, and then canonizing those boundaries as the essence of what proved to be a remarkably durable civilization, Byzantium managed to avoid the constant quarreling over the boundaries which characterized the western development. It did not, however, escape the unfortunate consequences which inevitably follow in the wake of such a confusion.

The practical effect of spiritualizing politics and politicizing religion—which is what the blurring or intertwining of the boundaries so often entailed—was that it became difficult for either church or state to pursue a course of action completely consistent with its own distinctive concerns and interests. There were, in fact, no truly distinctive interests in the Byzantine establishment. Maintaining political order in the realm of creation, which was avowedly the rationale for the state, meant, simultaneously, promoting and implementing the redemptive goals of the church. Maintaining spiritual order in the realm of redemption, on the other hand, which was avowedly the rationale for the church, meant, simultaneously, promoting and implementing the political goals of the state.

There are some, to be sure, who find the Byzantine model of church-state relations quite attractive. This is particularly true of those who believe that too rigid a separation between church and state leads to a compartmentalization of life or to an attitude of indifference with respect to the implications one realm has for the other. Why shouldn't the state promote the interests of the church? Why shouldn't the church, in turn, promote the interests of the state? In Byzantium, at least, religion and politics were not so completely divorced that the Christian was either forced into a kind of schizophrenia in order to participate in both realms or was compelled to give exclusive allegiance to one or the other.

It is precisely the experience of the Byzantine model, however, which provides the necessary cautions against making a confusion of church and state the answer to these legitimate questions and concerns. Promoting the work of the church is, indeed, consistent with the nature and purpose of the state. The state does not, however, promote the work of the church by actually doing it or legislating about it, but by providing a context of freedom and noninterference for the church in which it can carry out its own distinctive mandate. The state's responsibility over against the church, in other words, is to let the church be the church. Such an arrangement is not only to the advantage of the church, which is then free to be itself, but also consistently serves the best interests of the state.

The latter point can be dramatically illustrated by a development in Byzantine history which was to have unending repercussions in the history of western civilization. Byzantium, as we have already indicated, did not experience a "fall" until the very close of the period under review in this study. What it did experience at crucial points in its history was the disaffection of large numbers of its subjects because of the strict identity between itself and the church, in this case what we will have to call the Orthodox Church. Those who were led to disassociate themselves schismatically from the Orthodox Church, which was true of perhaps the majority of subjects living in such important provinces of the empire as Egypt, Palestine, and Syria, had no recourse but to repudiate their allegiance to the political structure which was inextricably bound up with the Orthodox Church.

Although it is premature to expect to encounter religious liberty as we know it at this point in history, it is nevertheless true that the best interests of the Byzantine state were not served by its confusion with a system of belief that had become unacceptable to many of its subjects. If the state had permitted the church to be the church by recognizing its independent rights and status, it could have more easily absorbed other systems of belief whose right to exist must always be the corollary of the church's freedom.

If we turn now to the question of the church promoting the work of the state, once again it can be said that such a promotion is entirely consistent with the nature and purpose of the church. Following the same principle applicable to the state, however, the church in its promotion of the state does not seek to do the work of the state or use the state to accomplish its distinctive goals and interests. The church best promotes the work of the state when it insists that the state be the state, the realm, that is, in which the functions and concerns peculiar to the state are effectively carried out.

The moment we begin to define what these functions and concerns are which the church should actively promote, we become involved in making theological judgments from an admittedly partisan point of view. Still, there is enough historical experience and evidence to suggest that the broadest and most commonly accepted theological definition—that the function of the state is to provide and maintain civil order and justice— accurately reflects most political theory and practice and hence can be used with some objectivity in conducting our analysis.

In the light of this definition, it should be noted, the church's confusion with the state is clearly brought into question. The state, quite simply, has a totally different function to perform, a function which belongs within a completely different frame of reference from the one which underlies the church's function and purpose. If there is to be any integrity to the state's administration of civil order and justice, it must be as free within its frame of reference to pursue those concerns as the church is in the pursuit of the interests peculiar to it.

This does not mean, as many have concluded, that the church must forever remain a disinterested bystander and let the state conduct its affairs, however arbitrarily, without any kind of critical review. If anything, a church that insists on the separate integrity of the state and its function should have an even greater reason to interest itself in the life of the state, simply because it should always find itself looking to see if the state is truly fulfilling its purpose. Is the state, in fact, providing civil order—meaningful and humane order? More importantly, perhaps, is it dispensing justice—true justice, open and available to all? In answering these questions, the church does not import its own special interests and frame of reference into the affairs of state; it does not try to turn the state into a church. Rather, it tries to help the state become what it is meant to be.

The Byzantine experience once again provides an instructive commentary on a relationship between church and state that mingles or confuses the two realms. Instead of enhancing the political order, as the apologists for Byzantium would have us believe, the church's virtual equation of itself with the state had the practical effect of removing the administration of civil order and justice from the church's critical review or concern. Having invested the political order with all the characteristics of a sacred mission through its total identification with the state, the Byzantine church was led to assume that the eternal value of this sacred mission would adequately encompass and fulfill the temporal needs of society. Anticipating the conditions of heaven more often became the church's program for the state than meeting the expectations of life on earth.

As the case of Byzantium amply attests, it simply is not true that a "Christianized" state necessarily leads to a more humane or just society. The legitimate concerns of life in this world are, in fact, easily overlooked or misrepresented by a church that confuses its interests with those of the state. A state, in turn, which is permitted to believe that the sacred authority of the church underlies and reenforces its activities runs the risk of claiming a finality for itself and its policies, a finality which, in practice, rules out the continual, pragmatic adjustments that are needed in the life of a state to keep it faithful to its reason for existence.

Thus, if one looks for the creative interplay between religion and politics in the Byzantine confusion of church and state, the search will end in disappointment. The distinctive functions and concerns of both church and state were so diluted by this confusion that no such creative interplay could take place. What resulted from the spiritualizing of politics and the politicizing of religion was a remarkably durable society, but a society marked nonetheless by acute symptoms of both political and ecclesiastical stagnation. When nature and grace are mixed—which is essentially what the Byzantine model of church-state relations attempted to do—neither is free to be itself, and both are compromised in their operation.

Much of what we have seen in the Byzantine experience will reappear from time to time in western church-state relations during the Middle Ages, but always with an important difference. The West will never be able to escape the tension which was built into its pattern of historical development, a tension which prevented a confusion of church and state from being hardened into a permanent solution as it was in the East. It is to that development, which was, of course, much more important for the formation of the American tradition of church-state relations than the eastern development, that we now must turn.

The Western Experience

Shortly after the legendary fall of Rome in the West—or, better yet, in the very midst of what that fall signified or represented—a Roman bishop by the name of Gelasius (A.D. 492–496) wrote a letter to the Byzantine emperor (who technically still ruled over the western or "fallen" half of the empire) complaining about the state's interference in the affairs of the church. This letter which went on to claim a totally separate authority and function for the church became a kind of declaration of independence for the medieval church, a document which would be invoked whenever the church was in danger of being swallowed up or controlled by the state. The Gelasian theory, or the doctrine of the Two Swords as it was popularly called, insisted that both church and state have their legitimate, divinely appointed spheres of influence, and that neither should be permitted to infringe upon or usurp the unique prerogatives of the other.

Historians generally agree that Gelasius' declaration of independence simply articulated something that was already a reality in the West, or was, at least, becoming increasingly possible. His letter was, in effect, a reminder to the Byzantine emperor that his political authority, along with all other forms of political authority in the West, was largely impotent and could not prevent the church from extracting itself from secular domination and manipulation. Although the church's sword (i.e., its authority) was not to be wielded physically or politically, events had transpired to make that sword a formidable weapon in the church's negotiations with the state, and Gelasius knew it.

To get a feeling for the extent and character of the political vacuum which Gelasius' declaration of independence presupposed, one need only refer to other letters by the same bishop which describe a political landscape virtually unbroken by anything resembling an orderly or effective administration. From other sources coming out of the same period, it is possible to see the shock-waves of Rome's fall extending into every area of life traditionally within the custody of the state. Education, for instance, not only went into decline but practically disappeared as an organized enterprise. The legal establishment which was responsible for defining and administering a cohesive system of justice largely vanished. Economic life reverted to unregulated and hence essentially chaotic conditions. Above all, however, the absence of law and order, at least in the sense in which they had been known during the happier days of the empire, became a major accent in the empire's decline and fall.

It is important to remember these conditions out of which the church made its bid for independence at the beginning of the medieval period, particularly as we seek to trace the way in which the church made use of that independence. To the great credit of the church, it responded to the political and social chaos of the times by picking up the broken pieces of the empire.

Many of the concerns of the state which were forfeited as a result of the empire's collapse were brought within the scope of the church's concern. Thus, education was to survive in the church, if nowhere else. Legal expertise was to be kept alive in the church's juridical system. Economic life was frequently forced to look to the church for what little regulation and guidance it could hope to receive. Even law and order were made to depend upon the good offices of the church. Indeed, in many provinces of the empire there was a continuity in civil administration only because the church with its more vibrant organizational structure absorbed many of the functions normally carried out by the state.

But this filling of the vacuum by the church—for which we should be grateful—also contained ominous significance for the history of church-state relations in the West. Gelasius' sword, which had been used to establish the independence of the church over against the state, had now become heavily encrusted with affairs which in more stable times properly belonged to the state. The church increasingly found itself in a kind of rivalry with the state. The church not only got a taste for independence in the chaotic situation that existed at the beginning of its medieval development; it also got a taste for worldly power and influence. It discovered that it could use the forfeited functions and activities of the state to promote its own temporal ambitions in this world.

If the church had designs on becoming a superstate, however, it was all rendered academic by the fact that the authority of the state ultimately revived in western Europe. The story of this revival in case after case will be the attendant discovery on the part of the state that many of its most important concerns, as well as the structures which supported and administered those concerns, were in the hands of the church.

This, in short, was the situation that dominated church-state relations throughout much of the Middle Ages—a church, on the one hand, which in the process of declaring its independence of the state, had overextended its boundaries so as to include large segments of the political order; and a state, on the other, which was determined to recover its political birthright, even if it had to be at the expense of the church's independence.

Given the peculiar dynamics which went into the western development, much of the energy spent on resolving the church-state issue was channeled into attempts to disentangle the interests and concerns peculiar to each sphere. Unlike the East which opted for a mingling of church and state, the West found itself continually engaged in trying to separate the two. There were, to be sure, other factors which contributed to this work of disentanglement; in our next chapter we shall see how a particular theological tradition in the West served to underscore and in some respects complicate the separate and independent interests of church and state. Still, the crucible in which the development of medieval church-state relations began—the crucible which dictated that tension would be an enduring dynamic in the western experience—left an indelible imprint on this development and continues to have important implications for church-state relations down to the present day.

CHURCH AND STATE IN COMPETITION

We began our last chapter by calling attention to an event which not only has impressive commemorative credentials of its own, but also occupies a prominent place in the history of church-state relations. Without having to resort to fantasy, we can begin this chapter, too, with an event from out of the distant past—an event which, once again, has impressive commemorative credentials of its own in the year 1976, and which, rather remarkably, also occupies a position of prominence in the history of relations between church and state.

In the year 1076—exactly nine hundred years ago—a Roman bishop by the name of Gregory VII excommunicated and deposed the Germanic or Holy Roman Emperor by the name of Henry IV. The act of deposition itself—which has always been regarded as one of the most blatant displays of papal pretensions in the Middle Ages—reads as follows: "I [i.e., Gregory] withdraw the government of the whole kingdom of the Germans and of Italy from Henry the King. . . . For he has risen up against the church with unheard of arrogance. And I absolve all Christians from the bond of the oath which they have made to him or shall make. And I forbid anyone to serve him as King."[1]

It is instructive, first of all, to contrast this deposition of an emperor representing a revitalized state in the West with the deposition with which we began our study of church-state relations in the last chapter. The deposition of Romulus Augustulus, the last of the Roman emperors in the West, signified the bankruptcy of Roman administration in the West, and made possible, as we noted in the previous chapter, the church's successful bid for independence from the state, as well as its subsequent appropriation of many of the functions and activities belonging to the political order. Now, in the events of 1076, we see this development being radically and dramatically challenged.

1. *Documents of the Christian Church*, ed. H. Bettenson (New York: Oxford, 1954), p. 146.

Henry IV was not content to accept the relationship between church and state which had evolved to a significant extent out of the breakdown of Roman order. As the head of what was believed to be a revival of the empire, he insisted on taking back those areas of administration and oversight which had formerly belonged to the state. In the process, he was led to challenge the very independence of the church, since the church's separate and independent rights were now so thoroughly mixed up with political matters. As Henry demanded control over more and more of the church's rights and privileges—some of which clearly infringed upon the prerogatives of the state, but others of which properly belonged to the church—he encountered louder and more threatening protests from Gregory. Finally, the tension between the two could no longer be contained, and church-state relations exploded in the anathema which Gregory pronounced on Henry and his "unheard of arrogance."

In a sense, Gregory's act may be described as a wistful attempt to restore the conditions under which the church had lived at the time of Romulus Augustulus' deposition. The church at that time was free to assume practical control over the affairs of the state because there was, in fact, no real king to be served; government had, in effect, "withdrawn" from the whole kingdom of the West. But Gregory was not dealing with a Romulus Augustulus. Henry IV was not a symbol of political vacuum but an able champion of the authority and rights of the state. Therein lay the unavoidable conflict between pope and emperor; and yet, curiously, therein also lay the potential for a creative and meaningful synthesis of the conflicting views which turned church and state into hostile camps.

The Theological Background

Before we look at how this most memorable of medieval conflicts between church and state was resolved, it is necessary to examine in some detail the mentality and theology that accompanied Gregory's desperate act in 1076. It certainly is not true, as many have insisted about Gregory, that his deposition of Henry was motivated by a lust for power or personal gain. On the contrary, he was completely sincere in his belief that what he was doing was for the best interests of both church and state.

If Gregory claimed the right to make and unmake emperors, which is to say the right to control when necessary the actual conduct of political affairs, it was because he believed that, apart from an incessant, benevolent monitoring of the state by the church, the state would pervert and destroy itself—something that he was convinced had already occurred under Henry and therefore required his drastic intervention. In Gregory's own mind, control of the state was never undertaken for the sake of control. There were always "higher" interests which stood behind his extravagant claims over against the state, interests which he believed were uniquely represented by himself as pope. Although much of his behavior certainly smacks of political opportunism, it was, in reality, a theological commitment rather than personal or political loyalties that dictated his policy toward the state.

Throughout the history of church-state relations in the West, as we have seen them unfold up to this point in our study, one particular theological tradition was constantly at work, sometimes helping to shape the course and character of those relations, sometimes reenforcing a pattern which had already emerged. This tradition, a version of which was determinative for Gregory's attitude toward the state, grew out of the thought of the man commonly acknowledged as the greatest theological authority in the church of the Middle Ages, Augustine of Hippo. Augustine's thought had to be reckoned with in every area of the church's life and teaching, and that meant, not least of all, taking seriously what he had to say—or what it was presumed that he had to say—about the relationship between church and state.

Church and State in Augustine's City of God

Without question, Augustine would have been puzzled by the medieval church's use of his so-called political theories, particularly the theories that touched upon the relationship between the church and the state. He had developed these theories in a massive, somewhat disorganized book called the *City of God,* a book which was so complicated both in conception and execution that scholars have scarcely caught up with its real meaning yet. Like so many great books, Augustine's *City of God* was capable of being quoted in support of totally different points of view, in this case totally different points of view concerning the proper relationship between church and state. Still, there was one fundamental perspective, one theological point of view, that ran with complete consistency throughout the entire work. It was this perspective or point of view that was to be most often used—and indeed, abused—by the medieval church in its dealings with the state.

The basic assignment which Augustine accepted in the *City of God* was that of seeking a solution to what is, perhaps, the greatest riddle of human existence: is there any real, abiding purpose or meaning to life? What point of reference, if any, can be found outside our immediate experience of life that will provide some sense of purposeful direction to our existence? Augustine, as one might expect, found the answer to this riddle in the teachings of the church. God—specifically God as we know him in Christ—is the point of reference which makes sense out of human affairs. God, for Augustine, is not only responsible for human life and its history through creation, but he remains its ongoing significance and ultimate fulfillment. Apart from God, human history is what Shakespeare declared it to be: a tale told by an idiot . . . signifying nothing.

It was out of this theological interpretation of history that Augustine went on to develop what would appear to later interpreters to be a full-scale analysis of church and state and the proper relationship that should exist between the two. Augustine, it should be noted initially, detected in human life two diametrically opposed societies or "cities" as he called them, the one having God as its constant point of reference or inner rationale, and the other, man himself. Translating this into less philosophical language, Augustine wrote that one city—the City of God—was marked by a love of God to the contempt of itself. It was a city or society that arranged all of its affairs in accordance with God's will and purpose rather than any special, independent interests of its own.

The other city—the Worldly City—was marked by a love of itself to the contempt of God. Here, all things were arranged in accordance with the selfish purposes of the society itself. Selfishness, in fact, became for Augustine the leading characteristic of this society. Those who lived within it—which for Augustine included the majority of the human race—used themselves and their earthly ambitions as the point of reference for achieving self-fulfillment and meaning in life.

Among the things to be emphasized about the foregoing analysis is the fact that neither the word "church" nor the word "state" was used. Although this was to become one of the most misunderstood aspects of Augustine's thought—a misunderstanding which would, in turn, seriously complicate church-state relations—Augustine nowhere neatly equates the City of God with the church; the church, that is, as a visible, earthly institution. The City of God as it is present in this life is always present in an interior way, in motive and outlook, rather than in external organization and structure.

There is, to be sure, a relationship between the City of God and the institutional church. Those who participate in an interior way in the City of God will always be found within the institutional church, but the institution as institution is not coextensive with the true church or City of God. The institutional church, in fact, actually belongs within the orbit of the Worldly City insofar as it includes many who do not genuinely share the religious outlook and orientation that constitute the real basis for membership in the City of God.

The last observation clearly suggests that even as the church as institution cannot be equated with the City of God neither can the state as institution be equated with the Worldly City. Here, again, it is an interior disposition or outlook on life that Augustine is talking about, not a formal structuring or organizing of society. As in the case of the City of God and the institutional church, there is once again a relationship between the Worldly City and the organized state. It is this relationship that we must now carefully investigate, for it was precisely at this point that Augustinian political theory had its greatest impact on medieval church-state relations. Whether transmitted in a distorted or more authentic version of his thought, Augustine's linking of the Worldly City with the state was to prove fateful for the discussion and resolution of church-state affairs.

The key to the relationship between the Worldly City and the state in Augustine's thought is the selfishness that dominates every aspect of life in the Worldly City. His view of this society is that it would be a kind of jungle if it was not regulated or controlled in some fashion. Living by the creed of "what's in it for me," the inhabitants of this society would destroy each other in the pursuit of their own selfish goals unless some restraints were placed on their activities. The function of the state in this particular context is, quite simply, to provide the restraints which an inveterately selfish human race needs merely to maintain its existence and effect some degree of order which will permit a variety of selfish interests to coexist.

The Negative Legacy of Augustine's City of God

This, quite obviously, ends up being a very negative view of the state. The state's only real justification for existence is the fact of human sinfulness, a point that was not lost on the medieval church as it looked for a justification of its own for taking control of so many affairs traditionally managed by the state. If the state exists only or even primarily to restrain sin, then why not let the institution which knows and, in fact, defines what sin is determine how and where these restraints should be administered? This is one of the attitudes that is regularly reflected in medieval church-state relations. Augustine's negative view of the state's purpose and function did not encourage doing away with the state altogether; the state had to exist in order to apply the actual restraints necessary to curb sin. With such a minimal charter, however, the state had little reason to concern itself with the scope or justice of its restraints. The church could do that so much better, not only because it was in control of the ideological presuppositions upon which the state's restraining function depended, but also because the church, throughout much of the Middle Ages, had a virtual monopoly on the judicial and legal apparatus that must always be the foundation for a system of restraints.

Another attitude which can be traced back to Augustine's minimal view of the state was one which closely paralleled the attitude just described, but was even more negative in its assessment of the role and function of the state. In this particular version of the Augustinian tradition, it was taken for granted that the state was contaminated by the selfishness or sinfulness of the society it was expected to regulate and restrain. By contagion, the state invariably became a support system for the self-serving designs of the Worldly City rather than a corrective of those designs. The state was, in fact, simply the sinful lust of the Worldly City in organized form. It would be unrealistic, according to this view, to look for justice—true justice—from the state, since the state was as infected by the jungle mentality and contempt for righteous conduct as the society whose interests the state was supposed to adjudicate.

Parenthetically, and yet appropriately, we can observe that we are in touch here with a part of that tradition in western European and American thought that regards politics as an essentially "dirty" business. Somewhere in that tradition will always be found the cynicism about the state that characterized Augustinian political theory in its most negative form—a cynicism that Augustine himself underscored when he declared that every state is simply an organized (and hence legitimized) band of robbers.

More to the point, however, we are also in touch here with the mentality and theology which dictated Gregory VII's policy in his dramatic showdown with the empire. If we tried to defend Gregory earlier from the charge that he was nothing more than an unscrupulous, opportunistic politician, it was because of our belief that his policy was much more a reflection of his sincere commitment to the theological presuppositions we have just described than an expression of any political ambitions he may have had. The fact that these theological presuppositions conveniently supported the considerable political power and prestige the church had managed to attain is not, of course, unimportant; but for Gregory himself such considerations were clearly secondary to the conclusions which his theological commitment forced upon him.

What were these conclusions which Gregory was forced to draw about the state? In brief, his conviction that the state was heavily implicated in the cupidity and self-serving activities of secular society led him to conclude that the state required a monitoring or restraining of its own. It could not be expected to promote justice and civil order if left to its own devices. Only by submitting to the church—a church which now spoke on behalf of the City of God through the papal office—could the state hope to fulfill the purpose it was meant to serve.

Failure to observe this arrangement between church and state could only result in the state reverting to the sinful instincts of the society which it represented, a reversion which, in Gregory's mind, was exemplified by the behavior of Henry IV. In terms of Gregory's theological outlook, Henry was an acute symptom of a chronic disease from which the state suffered. The church not only had the responsibility of trying to keep this disease under control, but had the unassailable right to intervene with drastic measures—including deposing the head of state—when the disease reached the crisis stage.

For Gregory, the crisis stage was reached when Henry refused to accept the position of dependency or tutelage which Gregory's view of the state presupposed. We can become so blinded by the specific issues under dispute in 1076 that we forget that any number of issues could have produced the same crisis. At stake here for Gregory were more than isolated areas of ecclesiastical jurisdiction, important as those areas were in and of themselves. The real danger in Henry's behavior was the unmistakable note of self-sufficiency or independent competence that ran throughout it. Henry was, in effect, declaring that the state no longer needed the church to authenticate and justify its existence. The state had a life of its own, and was fully competent to pursue its destiny without the paternalistic monitoring of its activities by the church.

The Positive Legacy of Augustine's City of God

Let us turn now to the other party in the dispute. Henry was an unusually gifted and forceful medieval statesman. He was not only restive about the degree of control which the church had come to assume over the affairs of the state, but was also determined to get out from under the theological system that complemented and legitimized that control. Increasingly throughout the Middle Ages, as the fortunes of the state revived, it was found necessary to challenge the negative view of the state which was imbedded in the Augustinian tradition. Politics, not as a desperate attempt to sublimate the baser instincts of mankind, but as a positive, creative force for promoting beneficial order and discipline in this world became the goal of many of these statesmen. This, as much as anything, was the source of the conflict between Gregory VII and Henry IV.

It is ironic that the development of a more positive attitude toward the state and its functions should also have been facilitated by the thought of Augustine. We cannot trace this development in any detail but shall only call attention to the ruler whose use of Augustine to magnify the importance of the state set an example which would be followed again and again by future rulers.

This ruler, known to all of us as Charlemagne, totally ignored the side of Augustine's thought that tended to implicate the state in the injustice and selfishness of the Worldly City, and chose to emphasize, instead, the divinely appointed role which the same Augustine had assigned to the state in preserving peace and order in the world. Instead of finding the origins of the state in the fact of human sinfulness, Charlemagne preferred to view the state as a reflection of God's benevolent purpose for mankind. The state, in other words, did not owe its existence to the incurable selfishness of the human race—a view which insured that the state would have an essentially minimal, restraining function—but to the natural, social order of things—a view that made the state a necessary dimension of the God-given structure for preserving and enhancing social life in this world.

Using such a rationale, Charlemagne went on to make claims about the state which would have left Augustine speechless. As the instrument for achieving God's social or political purpose for mankind, the state, Charlemagne believed, could approximate or perhaps even become Augustine's venerable City of God, particularly if the state were inseparably linked, through the church, with the spiritual ideals that constituted that City. Charlemagne took it for granted that, since both his foreign and domestic policies were expressions of his commitment to the values and objectives of the church, he had achieved, in earthly form, a realization of that Christian commonwealth which Augustine had made the key to human history.

The implications of this lofty view of the state for the question of church-state relations were momentous. Instead of being cast in the role of pupil or ward of the church, the state now became the patron of the church, defining and defending the church's supportive role in the state's fulfillment of its divine mission. For Charlemagne, the church was always one of the ministries or departments of government, having, to be sure, certain distinctive rights with which he did not actively interfere, but nevertheless clearly responsible to him in terms of its institutional life. Control over the church was as basic to the Carolingian version of Augustine's thought as control over the state was to the version represented by Gregory VII.

Charlemagne's understanding of the relationship between church and state is, of course, strongly reminiscent of the Byzantine solution. The same blurring or confusing of boundaries between church and state which we noted as a deliberate ideal in the case of Byzantium became the leading characteristic of the Carolingian settlement. If anything, the degree of "caesaropapism" in Charlemagne's empire was greater than it was in the East, for the simple reason that Charlemagne's conception of control did not allow for the reciprocity that was built into the

Byzantine model of church-state relations. If Charlemagne blurred the boundaries between church and state it was for the purpose of having those boundaries come under a single, unified leadership: his own.

Still, there is a crucial difference between this western confusion of church and state and its Byzantine prototype. The difference is to be found in that dynamic of tension to which we have referred so often, the dynamic which we are now in a position to see was reenforced by a variety of factors. In addition to the historical situation itself which had promoted a tradition of independence as well as considerable ecclesiastical imperialism in the medieval church, there was a theological tradition which seemingly pulled two ways and could not be invoked by one side of the church-state partnership without being challenged by the presuppositions and commitments of the other.

Consequently, when Henry IV sought to assert himself in the spirit of Charlemagne's ambitious, positive conception of political authority—as he appears deliberately to have done—he was instantly checked by the limitations which Gregory's commitment imposed on that authority. Henry's concern for the integrity of the state was as suspect to Gregory as Gregory's concern for the integrity of the church was to Henry. The two were, quite simply, at opposite poles of the tension which was inherent in the western development of church-state relations. From Gregory's point of view, the tension could be resolved only by excommunicating and deposing Henry, the sinner. From Henry's point of view, the tension could be resolved only by imprisoning and, in effect, sentencing Gregory, the subversive, to death.

The Medieval Struggle and Its Abiding Significance

If we have used this incident as a kind of case-study, it is because it illustrates so dramatically a perennial issue in church-state relations, not only in the Middle Ages but in the subsequent western—including the American—experience as well. The tragedy of Gregory and Henry, as we have already hinted, was that both were so committed to a one-sided approach to the problem of church and state—an approach which dictated

53

that one or the other must dominate in the relationship between the two—that they were incapable of recognizing the real point of tension that must always exist between church and state. Underlying their quarrel, as well as almost every other quarrel in the history of church-state relations in the West, was an almost congenital uneasiness about either church or state exercising control over the other. The fact that neither of the polar views which precipitated the crisis between Gregory and Henry was able to gain a clear-cut victory is a testimony to the vitality of that deeply engrained tradition in western thought which refuses to permit either church or state to be swallowed up by the other.

This is not to say that both church and state have ceased trying, subsequent to the crisis of 1076, to vindicate the polar views which Gregory and Henry represented. Gregory's legacy, which we need to look at first, is to be seen wherever the church, in the name of a theological tradition which assesses life in this world largely in pessimistic terms, views the state as little more than an instrument for curbing sin.

In addition to the fact that such a view can easily lead to a theoretical if not practical control of political life by the church, it is representative of an ethos which has even more fundamental political consequences. If the "rights" of the state (and, by extension, the "rights" of the citizens of the state) are essentially sinful rights—rights, that is, which grow out of or merely reflect the natural, selfish orientation of human life—they become something to be repressed and restrained rather than encouraged and defended.

Gregory's theological commitment, it can be argued, would have made it difficult for him to endorse the rights to which the American Declaration of Independence appeals. In particular, the right to pursue happiness would have appeared to him as a dangerous concession to the selfish instincts of humanity. For Gregory, and for the theological tradition which he represents, it is really only the church which has the right—the inalienable right—to pursue happiness, for only in the church is it possible to be freed from the twisted outlook on life that turns every human pursuit or so-called right into a violation of someone else's rights.

Above all, the state should not be encouraged to cast itself in the role of protecting or championing the rights of its citizens, for, in doing so, it would merely be intensifying the moral and ethical flaw endemic to human society. Although it would be grossly unfair to hold Gregory personally responsible for every political system which has attempted to fulfill its purpose by curbing the rights of its citizens, it is nevertheless true that the attitude which he exemplified has helped to support and legitimize such systems.

There is, to be sure, a sensitive theological issues which is at stake in Gregory's attitude toward the state, an issue which we dare not dismiss too casually. From the church's point of view, the state does, indeed, preside over a sinful or "fallen" humanity. The natural, inalienable rights of which we speak so fondly are, from the church's perspective, riddled with self-serving ambitions and designs. The church, moreover, has every right to insist that happiness—true happiness—can be pursued and found only within the context of its mission and message.

All of this pessimism about the quality of life in the political realm, however, does not give the church the right to fashion the state in the image of a fallen humanity. The state does not exist as a corollary of the church's pessimistic evaluation of human society, but as an expression of God's will. Restraining "sinners" (which includes, of necessity, curtailing the selfish interests of its citizens) is, to be sure, an important function of the state, but given the frame of reference in which the state operates—the preservation of God's creation, under the law—this function can and should be stated more positively.

In addition to being a threatening instrument which punishes injustice, the state must also be an instrument of promise through its championing of justice. Although it can do nothing to effect the righteousness that "saves" in a redemptive sense, it has the responsibility to advance and uphold the righteousness that dignifies God's creation through an equitable and humane management of earthly affairs.

Seen from this more positive, political perspective, the rights of man become something more than testimonies to the ego-centricity of the human race. They are, in short, what the Declaration of Independence declared them to be: political birth-rights. As a part of God's creation, we are born with the right to pursue a life in this world which is consistent with the dignity and equity inherent in his creative purpose. The function of the state is nothing more and nothing less than that of nurturing and protecting those rights.

It would be gratuitous to suggest that all of the political principles just outlined were endorsed by Henry IV in his quarrel with the church. As we did in the case of Gregory and the tradition which he represented, we must now look briefly at the legacy—the unfortunate legacy—which Henry's one-sided use of a more positive attitude toward the state has had in the history of church-state relations. Perhaps the simplest way of detecting this legacy is provided by the many instances in the western experience of what may be called the domestication of the church by the state. In essence, this was what Henry did or tried to do, convinced as he was that the church as an institution was something to be used by the state in fulfilling its all-embracing political task. Whenever the church is "bridled" by the state in such a way that it becomes an instrument for carrying out or propping up the totally comprehensive interests of the state, the policy of Henry IV may, in fact, be said to have been at least partially vindicated.

Once again, however, there was something more at stake in this one-sided approach to church-state relations than institutional control. For Henry, as well as for the tradition which was to emulate his attempt to domesticate the church, there was a constant temptation to believe that the moral and spiritual authority of the church rubbed off on any state that linked its political program so intimately with the work of the church.

In "Christian" Europe, and in more subtle ways, in "Christian" America, this tradition was to lead to the conceit that the state was the earthly expression of the Ciy of God. The state was not only the custodian of the proximate concerns of God's creation, but became the embodiment of or substitute for the ultimate concerns of God's redemption. In some versions of this tradition, the church was not even necessary; indeed, God was not necessary. Having discovered that it could domesticate the institution which was the vehicle for the ultimate concerns of life, the omnicompetent, totally comprehensive state discovered that it could domesticate the ultimate concerns themselves.

That the church should and usually does register alarm when confronted with such a solution to the church-state problem is, of course, quite obvious. What is not always so obvious, however, is what the primary concern of the church should be in such a situation. Gregory tended to make the institutional integrity of the church his primary concern, an integrity that resisted the pretensions of the state by making a counterclaim of finality and unlimited authority for the institutional church. What he failed to realize is that the church can no more become an embodiment of the "ultimacy" to which the church testifies than the state can. The church has no greater right to domesticate the sovereign reference point of history within its institutional walls than the state has. It is not for the sake of those walls that the church protests against a state or political system that makes ultimate or "churchly" claims about itself, but for the sake of the gospel of Jesus Christ. For the church, the gospel is the true wall of separation between human attempts to counterfeit ultimate meaning through political action and God's vindication of ultimate meaning through the cross and resurrection.

In the next chapter we will have occasion to examine in greater detail the church's confrontation with a state that claimed too much for itself. For now, we need only call attention once again to the peculiarly western restiveness that has prevented this particular one-sided solution, as well as the solution which claimed too much for the church, from being hardened into a permanent pattern of church-state relations.

The struggle between Gregory and Henry, representing as it does two extremes in the development of those relations, is a forceful reminder of the importance of that historical and theological tendency which we have called the dynamic of tension.

On the one hand, we can applaud Gregory and his insistence on the freedom of the church. His attempts to use that freedom as a means of controlling the life of the state cannot, however, be endorsed without running the risk of compromising the authority and integrity of both church and state. Henry, on the other hand, can similarly be applauded for his attempt to liberate the state from ecclesiastical domination. His inability to recognize the limits of that liberation, however, provides a constant warning to both church and state that a too ambitious assertion of political prerogatives can easily become a tyrannical denial of religious privileges.

In so many ways, our own political and religious heritage is a reflection and an expression of the tension—the healthy tension—that is implicit in the quarrel between these two men, a quarrel which rather remarkably observes its "Novicentennial" —its nine hundreth anniversary—in the same year in which a nation which has dedicated itself to the separation of church and state celebrates its Bicentennial.

CHURCH AND STATE IN CONFLICT

The United States of America has a long way to go before it can celebrate an anniversary as outstanding as the one which the city of Rome celebrated in A.D. 247. In that year, Rome observed its millennium, the one thousandth anniversary of its legendary foundation. Although the records concerning this observance are scanty, we can assume that it was marked by great festivity and splendid ceremonies, not only in the city of Rome itself but throughout Rome's far-flung empire as well.

From everything that we know about the situation at that time, however, there was one group, one large segment of the population, that did not participate in Rome's millenary celebrations. This group—which, today, we would probably call a disaffected or alienated minority—had a long history of strained relations with the Roman state. Sometimes used as a scapegoat by Roman society, sometimes persecuted as an unprofitable and fundamentally disloyal ideology by the state itself, this group had ample reason for disassociating itself from the festivities and ceremonies which glorified Rome's earthly accomplishments.

The group to which we refer was, of course, the Christians, a group which, while still a minority at the time of Rome's millennium, had grown into a movement of empire-wide significance. To get a feeling for the numerical proportions of the estrangement represented by the early Christians, we might compare them with a sizable minority in our society, the blacks. The parallels between the early Christians and black America extend, in fact, beyond mere population percentages. Much of the same sense of alienation which the early Christians felt upon the occasion of Rome's millennium can be discovered in black America's reaction to the celebration of our Bicentennial. The early Christians, quite simply, found little with which they could identify in Rome's self-congratulatory festivities. They had little reason to extol a state which had not only denied them their dignity as Christians but was dedicated in so many respects to a totally different set of ideals and values than the ones to which they had committed themselves.

The relationship of the early Christians to the Roman state prior to the conversion of Constantine (when the state's hostility toward Christianity gave way to toleration and eventually favoritism) is one that has held great romantic interest for Christians in every subsequent age. Living as they did under the constant threat of persecution by the state, these early Christians have been invested with the kind of heroism that belongs to a departed, Golden Age—an age that we are fond of recalling but which has little in common with present reality. Supposedly we can learn constancy and self-sacrifice from the example of these heroic witnesses to the faith, but never under quite the same conditions as those which served to test their faith. They, after all, were confronted by a state which penalized them, even to the point of putting them to death, for their religious convictions. Except in isolated instances today, Christians no longer face the problems that elicited the church's response to the state in that age of saints and martyrs.

We have not, in fact, outgrown the conditions—the fundamental conditions—which served to throw the early church's relationship to the state into such heroic relief. Its basic attitude toward the state is as relevant today as it was upon the occasion of Rome's millennium. Its response to the state deserves careful study by Christians in every age, not as a historical curiosity but as a perennial option in the church's ongoing attempt to establish a proper and meaningful relationship with the political order.

Rome's Abuse of Power

Of all the complaints which the early church had against the Roman state, the one which voiced its disaffection most succinctly was the charge that Rome claimed too much for itself. For all but a relatively small group of militants who wrote Rome off altogether as an inherently satanic empire, the early Christian indictment of Rome was based most frequently upon what was believed to be an abuse of political power by the state, an abuse which led, in turn, to a perversion of the state's legitimate role and function. The fact that the state persecuted the church was simply a confirmation of its abuse of power and perversion of purpose. A state that lived in accordance with its true mandate would not persecute a group which was as beneficial to society as the early Christians believed themselves to be.

In a very real sense, the early church's struggle with the Roman state, which was always a struggle for the survival of the church, was also a struggle for the survival of the state, the state, that is, as a proper state which did not overextend its authority and thereby forfeit its right to govern. It is ironic, as well as immensely significant, that the group within Roman society which was perhaps the most alienated from the state was, at the same time, the group that showed the greatest concern about the state. Indeed, it is this peculiar dialectic of alienation and concern that makes the early church's attitude and response to the state so relevant in every historical situation, including our own.

Perhaps the best way of uncovering just what it was that the early Christians meant when they charged Rome with claiming too much for itself is provided by an investigation of the state's repressive policy toward the church. We automatically assume that since Rome persecuted the Christians it was an intolerant state which permitted only one form of religious belief and expression which we vaguely call "paganism." In actual fact, Rome was an unusually tolerant state when it came to religious matters. It sheltered an incredibly wide variety of religious systems and cults under its leadership. Except for the devotees of some of the more bizarre cults which violated the most elementary standards of civilized life, the subjects of Rome were surprisingly free to practice the religion of their choice.

Why, then, did the church come into conflict with this state which for its own time was a veritable paragon of religious liberty? If the question seems to be a natural one for us to ask, it was even more natural for the Roman state to ask the question. Why, indeed, did the Christians refuse to live within the generous religious environment which the Roman state created and maintained?

Aside from the outright calumnies which from time to time made Christians vulnerable to persecution, this was the very issue that lay behind the state's policy—its generally reluctant policy—of repression of the church. Exasperated by the church's stubborn refusal to adapt itself to its paternalistic system, the Roman state found that it had no recourse but to deny the Christians the very thing that they seemed unwilling to accept. As much as anything, Christians were persecuted for their stubbornness in the face of what Rome believed to be a most enlightened and liberal management of religious matters.

At times, to be sure, their stubbornness was believed to veil subversive activities within the church. On such occasions, persecution, which was most frequently experienced by Christians in rather subtle forms, gave way to outbreaks of violence against the church. Even then, however, when Christians were actually being put to death, the state found its greatest source of irritation in the Christians' obstinate refusal to subsume their religious pursuits under the benevolent agenda of the Roman order.

One cannot help but be partially sympathetic to the Roman

state in reading the accounts of actual confrontations between the early Christians and the magistrates who represented the policy and interests of the state. In most instances, the tone of the confrontation from the side of the state is one of reasonableness, often approaching a kind of compassion. Unlike the romantic image of early Christian persecution which so many of us have, the church was not confronted by a sadistic monster which killed Christians as a form of entertainment. Normally, persecution in an overt form was something that the state undertook only as a last resort. Even then it made what can only be called humanitarian efforts to spare the Christians from the unfortunate consequences to which their obstinacy led.

Why, then, we must ask again—this time from the point of view of the church—did the early Christians come into conflict with the state? We have already found the answer to this question in the church's contention that the Roman state had claimed too much for itself. In the light of Rome's essentially reasonable and tolerant predisposition we must examine whether there was, in fact, any truth to this contention. If it is not true that the state was motivated by sadistic impulses in its treatment of the Christians, is it possible—as some have claimed—that the Christians were motivated by a kind of masochism in their defiant attitude toward the state? Was their stubborn opposition to the state merely a stratagem for insuring their persecution, or was it an expression of an intense religious commitment which was willing to accept persecution as a regrettable but unavoidable risk?

The Issue Is Ultimate Loyalty

The basic issue which was constantly being contested between the early Christians and the Roman state was precisely the intensity with which Christians were committed to the practice of their religion. Stated in slightly different terms, the issue was the relatively simple one of loyalty, specifically primary or ultimate loyalty. For the church, it was axiomatic that Christians could have only one ultimate loyalty which gave meaning and purpose to life and which determined the choice and character of every secondary loyalty to which Christians might be committed. This primary loyalty was artlessly expressed by the early Christians in the confession "Jesus Christ is Lord." This confession immediately brought them into conflict with the paternalistic pretensions of the Roman order.

No one saw more clearly than the early Christians that there was always a price that had to be paid in order to enjoy Rome's celebrated magnanimity. The price was the surrender of any loyalty that might transcend Rome's comprehensive claims on its subjects. Everything within the Roman order was expected to fall into place and find its meaning within the loyalty—the primary loyalty—which was due to the state. Given such an ordering of priorities, Jesus Christ could easily be absorbed into the Roman pantheon; any religious commitment was capable of being subsumed under Rome's ideological umbrella as long as Rome's interests were made of paramount concern. To acknowledge Christ as Lord, however, and mean it, was to challenge the lordship claimed by the state. It was to make religious conviction more important than political conformity.

This, in essence, was the source of the quarrel between the early church and the Roman state. For the church, Christ was the ruling perspective for all of life; for Rome, the state was the comprehensive authority that must absorb all other perspectives.

The point at which the contradictory loyalties of church and state was contested most sharply and dramatically was the act or ceremony designated somewhat misleadingly as emperor worship. This act which often became a part of the judicial proceedings against Christians did not, as is commonly thought, have as its main object the worship of the Roman emperor as god. Christians, in fact, were informed by the magistrates that they could, in effect, keep their fingers crossed when they swore by the genius of Caesar and offered incense before his image.

What Christians were not permitted, however, were any reservations about the absolute priority of Rome's interests and claims. If acknowledging the divinity of the emperor was a matter of personal taste, acknowledging the divinity of the state, of which the emperor was the visible symbol, was an inescapable requirement for everyone. This was the real purpose served by so-called emperor worship: it was primarily a test of one's basic loyalty—a kind of loyalty oath—which served to assure the state that its lordship would not be diluted or compromised by any competing loyalties. It goes without saying, of course, that the early Christians rather consistently failed this test. They failed, not because they had taken an oath to obstinacy but because they had taken an oath to One who they believed stood above Rome and called all of its pretensions into question.

It is very important that we correctly identify what was really at stake in the early Christians' experience with emperor worship if we are to find any ongoing significance in their response. Although the church has occasionally been confronted by individuals who have demanded a kind of worship of themselves and their political genius, it is more common for the church to encounter what one writer calls an "apotheosis of power"[2]—a deification, in other words, of the comprehensive authority of the state.

Today, we normally label such a concentration and glorification of power "totalitarianism," a phenomenon which we tend to believe is of comparatively recent origin. As the experience of the early Christians demonstrates, however, Rome represented precisely such an apotheosis of power. Its obsession—which was the unconditional priority of all its interests and pursuits—is the obsession of every totalitarian state. If, then, totalitarianism—whether in a notorious or more subtle form—is a living concern in the contemporary world, as it most assuredly is, the relevance of the early Christian witness to an absolute state is underscored and enhanced.

Among other things, the witness of the early church should alert us to the fact that totalitarianism is not synonymous with the abolition or even persecution of religion. We cannot neatly equate the hard core of totalitarianism with the militant atheism of a political system like that of the Soviet Union. The totalitarian state, as the example of Rome attests, is equally capable of

2. Charles Norris Cochrane, *Christianity and Classical Culture* (New York: Oxford, 1957), p. 113.

encouraging and protecting religion—encouraging and protecting, that is, as long as religion is content to play a supporting role in the pursuit of the state's interests. It is, in fact, much more typical of the totalitarian state that it uses religion to authenticate and solidify its rule. The Nazi form of totalitarianism probably expressed the fundamental bias of the totalitarian state with respect to religion when it insisted on a complete "coordination" of religion with the programs and goals of the state.

Religion as a form of service to the state, which was essentially what Rome demanded, was clearly unacceptable to the early Christians. Equally unacceptable were Rome's efforts to coordinate the Christians' loyalty to Christ with the all-inclusive interests of the state. In addition to the fact that a coordination or harmonization of religious and political interests in a totalitarian state can never be anything more than a euphemism for state control, such a policy was predicated upon a view of religion which was totally foreign to Christianity.

As is true of most totalitarian states, Rome viewed religion as having two distinct dimensions or "faces." There was the private face of religion which involved what we might call "faith" or beliefs; it operated in a purely interior way, in the mind or heart, and had as its major concern the question of eternal destiny, or, as we might put it, the salvation of the soul. In addition to this private face, there was, or could be, a public dimension to religion which was to be seen any time a religion translated its interior commitments into public or social action.

In general, Rome was disinterested in the private face of religion. We completely misrepresent the Roman state and the experience of early Christianity if we think that Rome was bent upon destroying the faith—the private faith—of the church. If Christians wanted to believe in the madness about a crucified carpenter being the savior of their souls that was their private misfortune. They could even style him Lord if they chose— Lord, that is, of a purely spiritual, interior realm. When this acknowledgment of Christ as Lord began to spill over into their public lives, however, the Roman state became nervous.

For Rome, the public face of religion must be coordinated

with the organism that *is* the public, namely, the state. In this organism, there is no room for a lordship that supersedes or in any way qualifies the lordship of the state. The Christ who is blessed as Lord in private must be cursed in public. This was the inevitable outcome of Rome's policy of coordinating religion with the life of the state, an outcome, it must be noted, which was seen more clearly by the early Christians than by anyone else, including many of the "noblest" Romans who found the repression of the Christians a most distasteful and regrettable business.

Throughout the history of the church, Christians have been tempted to rationalize their religious identity along the lines suggested by the Roman policy. What we believe in private is our own affair; but what we do in public becomes the concern of the state and therefore must be coordinated or harmonized with the demands and policies of the state.

Christians need that clarity of vision which the early Christians possessed, when they refused to fragment their religious identity into private and public spheres. That vision is needed not only when the church is threatened by persecution, but even more, perhaps, when the church is confronted by a state which encourages even a public blessing of Christ as Lord as a political expedient. The early Christians could never have succumbed to a formula which makes the practice of religion—going to church, for instance—into a means of affirming and strengthening the state. For all of the political rhetoric that might accompany such a formula, the early church with its "seamless" loyalty to Christ would have seen it as a potentially dangerous compromise of Christ's lordship, a lordship which was supreme in every area of life, private and public, and which could not be relativized into a social or political prop.

The early Christians, in short, were unwilling to accept the notion that there are degrees to the lordship of Christ, depending on the context in which Christians find themselves. Their public expression of religion was as dominated by their commitment to Christ as their private lives. Whatever they did, they did for the sake of Christ, not for the sake of some other loyalty or cause.

As we noted earlier, this single-minded commitment to Christ resulted in a relationship between church and state which can best be characterized—from the church's side, at least—as one of alienation. We must be careful, however, when we make such a characterization that we do not intepret alienation to mean disinterest or apathy.

Another of the common misconceptions about the early church is that it was committed, as a matter of principle, to noninvolvement in public or secular affairs. The early Christians are often pictured as political and social dropouts who spent all their time cultivating otherworldly concerns. There were, to be sure, some Christians then, as there are now, who made alienation from the state and society a permanent and inflexible part of their life-style. For the vast majority of early Christians, however, life in the world was no less real and no less important than it is for us. If they were alienated from the world, it was because that world in its bondage to Rome's lordship was dedicated to ideals and values which they could not embrace.

If Christians withdrew from society, as they occasionally did, it was not out of indifference but out of concern. Rome's often-repeated charge that the Christians were unprofitable members of society who hated the human race was indeed true, but true only in terms of Rome's understanding of what was profitable for mankind.

Christian Commitment to the State

One of the most amazing spectacles in human history—which should be a source of unending pride to Christians—is this alienated church struggling to keep alive the very state which denied Christians a right to exist. The decline and fall of Rome to which we referred in our first chapter was not something that suddenly materialized in the fifth century. The seeds of Rome's fall can be found centuries earlier. During the period of Rome's persecution of the church, these seeds had, in fact, germinated to such an extent that the final fall could be predicted with almost complete certainty.

And yet, in the midst of the declining fortunes of the state, in the midst of the empire-wide malaise that made even the celebration of Rome's millennium a desperate display of bravado, there was one group—the Christians—who were trying to salvage the state. Their program for the survival of the state could not include, of course, a rededication to the glorious tradition of empire which had made Rome synonymous with power and authority. It was precisely that tradition which was the source of the Christians' alienation from the state.

Christian dedication went rather into efforts to transform the state into a proper state, a state which was not a monument to political arrogance, but an instrument of human justice and creativity. In essence, what the early church's program for the survival of the state called for was a relativizing of the absolute demands of the state—a rendering unto Caesar the things that were properly Caesar's—and a recognition of the right of all its subjects to render unto God the absolute, unconditional loyalty that belonged to God.

Normally, when we try to catalogue the ways in which the early Christians demonstrated a concern about the state, we come up with a list which consists of one entry: Christians prayed for the state. It is true that, in defending themselves against the charge that they were a subversive element in the Roman order, they frequently pointed to their prayers on behalf of the state as evidence to the contrary.

Without minimizing the importance of these prayers as an index to the positive attitude which the early church had toward the state, we need to look also at the quiet, almost instinctive way in which most Christians went about the task of keeping the state alive. Perhaps the modern expression "fifth column" comes as close as any to capturing the nature of the Christian presence in the Roman world. Although they were social and political outcasts, they infiltrated every activity and structure of the Roman order, trying to imbue life in this world with the dignity and value which their loyalty to Christ dictated.

It is important to note that the last and most serious persecution of the church by the Roman state was not undertaken because Christians had withdrawn from the sphere of influence commanded by the state. Instead, they had infiltrated it to such an extent that the state was in danger of losing its total control over the lives and destinies of its subjects. "Everywhere you look these days," one Roman statesman complained in so many words, "you see Christians trying to change things in accordance with their foreign ideology." The foreign ideology of the Christians, however, was not a new form of tyranny which was to be imposed as a comprehensive political settlement on an exhausted empire. It was rather a way of helping that empire regain its political soul, the soul it forfeited when it claimed too much for itself and tried to become the end of life rather than the means by which life—the good life here on earth—can be pursued.

The vitality and resolution that Christianity was helping to inject into the bloodstream of an ailing empire were not lost on the man who effected the greatest revolution in church-state relations in the history of the church. Historians have argued for centuries about why this man—the emperor Constantine— converted to Christianity and thereby ended the hostility which had existed between church and state since the beginning of the Christian mission. The question, admittedly, is a complicated one, but one thing about which we can be completely certain is that Constantine recognized in Christianity a force for renewal —political renewal—which was unavailable in the worn-out ideology of the Roman state.

Constantine's conversion, in order words, regardless of what it may or may not have meant in terms of actual religious conviction, was a testimony to the relevance of Christianity in the political realm, a relevance which he did not merely surmise but which had been demonstrated by the early Christians under the most trying circumstances. If nothing else will convince us that the most intense loyalty to Christ can be combined with participation in the affairs of the state, Constantine's decision to identify himself and his rule with the church should go a long way toward overcoming our reservations. It is inconceivable that a politician as shrewd as Constantine would have chosen for his ideological ally a religion which considered politics unclean or unworthy of Christian participation.

Every Christian today who chooses either to remain aloof from politics or insists on approaching politics with a different set of standards or values stands indicted by those Christians of an earlier age who were prepared to bleed—literally bleed—for a loyalty which at one and the same time compelled them to speak out in prophetic judgment against the state and yet immerse themselves completely in the search for a just and humane political order.

Under Constantine's protection of the church, the church was to inherit a whole new set of problems with respect to its relationship to the state. Some of these we have examined in the two previous chapters. In every historical situation, however, the witness of the early church remains a valuable reference point for Christians as they seek to understand the implications of their loyalty to Christ for their lives in this world.

We cannot express it better than an anonymous Christian from the early church who wrote:

> Christians cannot be distinguished from the rest of the human race by country or language or customs. They do not live in cities of their own; they do not use a peculiar form of speech; they do not follow an eccentric manner of life. . . . They have a share in everything as citizens, and endure everything as foreigners. Every foreign land is their fatherland, and yet for them every fatherland is a foreign land. They marry, like everyone else, and they beget children, but they do not cast out their offspring. They share their board with each other, but not their marriage bed. It is true that they are "in the flesh," but they do not live "according to the flesh." They busy themselves on earth, but their citizenship is in heaven.[3]

3. *Epistle to Diognetus,* ch. 5.

Gerhard A. Krodel

The Kingdom of Caesar and the Kingdom of God

"RENDER TO CAESAR THE THINGS THAT ARE CAESAR'S" AND "REPENT, FOR THE KINGDOM OF GOD IS AT HAND"

Christianity arose within the Roman Empire which by conquest and treaty had incorporated peoples and countries stretching from Spain to Armenia and from Britain to Egypt and North Africa. Rome was hailed as savior by those who benefited from its policy of law and order or who shared in its wealth and gained by the privileges which the new order bestowed on certain classes. The government's provisions of "bread and games" kept the urban proletariat content most of the time, and therefore it is not surprising that social unrest was limited in scope.

What Virgil's messianic eclogue proclaimed—namely, the coming of a new age of peace in which fear and hatred among peoples would cease—seemed to many inhabitants of the empire to have come to pass in the reign of Augustus, whose birthday was celebrated as "gospel" in Asia Minor. From the middle of the second century we hear a Greek rhetorician extolling in extravagant language the glory of Rome: "No envy sets foot in the empire. . . . Things as they are satisfy and benefit both poor and rich. . . . Cities shine in radiance and beauty. . . . Universal order and the bright light of life and government have come."[1]

1. These quotations from Aelius Aristides are found in an article by Clarence Lee, "Social Unrest and Primitive Christianity" in Benko-O'Rourke, *The Catacombs and the Colosseum. The Roman Empire as the Setting of Primitive Christianity* (Valley Forge: Judson Press, 1971), pp. 122–23.

Yet behind the glitter and facade of the empire, in spite of its policy of religious toleration and political pacification, there also existed a hatred of Rome within certain provinces and segments of the populace. Roman imperialism struck terror into those not yet conquered. What the Pax Romana meant to people outside the empire is well expressed by the words which Tacitus puts into the mouth of Galgacus, a Celtic chieftain.

> Even the sea is not safe, menaced as we are by a Roman fleet. . . . To us who dwell on the uttermost confines of the earth and of freedom, this remote sanctuary of Britain's glory has up to this time been a defence. . . . Beyond us are the terrible Romans from whose oppression escape is vainly sought by obedience and submission. Robbers of the world, having by their universal plunder exhausted the land, they rifle the deep. If the enemy be rich, they are rapacious; if he be poor, they lust for dominion; neither the East nor the West has been able to satisfy them. . . . To their robbery, slaughter and plunder they give the lying name of empire. They create a desert and call it peace.[2]

The Roman historian Dio Cassius who served as governor of Africa and Dalmatia, and hence knew what he was talking about, expressed without shame the imperialistic principle that "might makes right." For him, "No law is stronger than the law of armed might. The strongest power always gives the appearance of just words and actions."[3]

Hence it is not surprising that subjugated peoples on the borders of the empire were apt to revolt. Germanic tribes annihilated the three legions of Varus in A.D. 9. The Britons rebelled during the reign of Claudius. On the lower Danube, Rome faced one rebellion after the other. In North Africa bands of robbers, partisans, vented their hatred of Rome by taking up arms. The Jews of Judea rose up in two large-scale rebellions in A.D. 66 and 132, as did the diaspora Jews in North Africa and Cyprus in A.D. 115. For the Jews who participated in these revolts their desperate efforts against Rome's oppression were not only launched in order to gain political independence as we shall see

2. Tacitus, *Agricola*, 30.
3. Dio Cassius, *Nero*, 61.

later, but they surely were also caused by Roman oppression.

Since Christianity originated within the matrix of Judaism, we shall first try to understand the traditions toward foreign powers found in the Old Testament and in first century Judaism. Then we shall deal with the mission and message of Jesus who proclaimed the kingdom of God.

The Historical Context of Jesus' Ministry

The faith that God was to be king over his chosen people expressed itself politically in that Israel was a theocracy.[4] The amphictyony, later the state, was to be governed by Yahweh himself as its sole ruler, lawgiver, and judge.

Since David's time the earthly king was to be the viceroy of the heavenly king, dispensing Yahweh's justice over his people. But then came the great crises when Assyria and Babylonia conquered Israel and Judah. When these catastrophes engulfed the theocracy, when Yahweh's cause seemed irretrievably lost, then prophets interpreted them as punishment which God sent upon his people. Nebuchadnezzar of Babylon was Yahweh's "servant" (Jer. 27:5-7) to whom God surrenders the land for a period of time. The king of Babylon executes God's judgment. For the prophets it was unimportant that the pagan kings were unaware of their role as Yahweh's servants. The Persian king, Cyrus, was proclaimed by Deutero-Isaiah to be the "Lord's anointed" (Isa. 45:1 ff.), and in Daniel we read that God removes kings and installs kings and gives earthly thrones to whomever he wills (Dan. 2:21; 4:25).

While foreign rulers were usually denounced as idolators, or passively accepted as rods of Yahweh's wrath against his people (Isa. 10:5), Jeremiah went far beyond a mere negative attitude toward the pagan empire when he exhorted the exiles in Babylon: "Seek the welfare of the city where I have sent you into exile, and pray on its behalf; for in its welfare you will find your welfare" (Jer. 29:7). Here for the first time the pagan empire is no longer an object of hatred or resignation, and this attitude,

4. The word "theocracy" was coined by Josephus, *Against Apion,* 2, 165–66.

enunciated by Jeremiah, enabled Judaism to live in the diaspora also after the exile.

Philo of Alexandria, a contemporary of St. Paul, not only recalled imperial decrees which granted special privileges to the Jewish people, but also emphasized the obedience and loyalty of Judaism toward Caesar and his laws. On several occasions he speaks of the prayers which are rendered daily in synagogues on behalf of their Roman benefactors.[5] Through Josephus we hear that sacrifices for the well-being of the emperor and the benefit of the empire were offered twice daily in Jerusalem's temple.[6] The last prefect of the priesthood prior to the revolt of A.D. 66 exhorted the people: "Pray for the welfare of the government [meaning Rome] for if there were no fear of it we would have devoured each other already."[7]

Even Paul's statement in Romans 13 that "every man be subject to the governing authorities" has its antecedent in traditions of Hellenistic Judaism which held that no ruler attains his office save by the will of God. Because rulers have their office from God, therefore "fear the Lord and the king and do not disobey either of them" (Prov. 24:21), but rather show "unswerving loyalty" (2 Macc. 3:3). Rulers are "servants of his [God's] kingdom" (Wisd. of Sol. 6:3–4).

Submission and loyalty to the governing authorities would, of course, cease when apostasy was demanded. For instance, when the emperor Gaius in A.D. 39 ordered the erection of his statue in the temple at Jerusalem, then the Jews resisted, "presenting themselves, their wives and children ready for the slaughter."[8] However, as long as religious toleration was practiced by Rome, many Jews "rendered unto Caesar the things which are Caesar's."

Yahweh's lordship over the world and in history was then distinguished from his reign in Israel, his theocracy. He rules

---

5. Philo, *Embassy to Gaius,* 236, 280, 306, etc.

6. Josephus, *War,* II, 140, 197, etc.

7. G. F. Moore, *Judaism in the First Centuries of the Christian Era* (Cambridge: Cambridge University Press, 1950), vol. 2, p. 114.

8. Josephus, *War,* II, 197.

over history because he is the Creator of heaven and earth (Jer. 27:5), but he rules over Israel through his Torah. When Jews recited the *Shema,* Deut. 6:4 ff., they meant to "take the yoke of the kingdom of heaven upon" their shoulders by keeping the law. God's reign occurred in the present when a man submitted to the Torah and in so doing he established the kingdom of God. Hence, the kingdom was thought to be a Torah-structured kingdom. Its precepts and prohibitions contain the revelation for the whole of life, regulating all aspects of personal and communal existence.

Moreover, first century Judaism spoke of yet a third form of God's reign. His kingdom was to be established in the future. The eschatological expectations of the contemporaries of Jesus varied greatly. Some contemporaries of Jesus expected a reversal of the national fortunes from a Davidic Messiah who would "destroy the godless nations" and rule in the power of the "Holy Spirit" over a renewed nation (Psalms of Sol. 17).

Political quietists could prepare for the coming kingdom through works of piety. In prayer Yahweh was besought: "Sound the trumpet for our freedom. . . . May the arrogant kingdom [Rome] soon be rooted out in our days."[9] Works of piety or obedience toward the Torah were thought not merely to assure personal reward by God, but also to hasten the coming of Yahweh's future kingdom. It is this notion of cooperating with God which united the political quietists, the Pharisees and their kin, with the political revolutionaries, the Zealots, who wanted to usher in the kingdom of God through rebellion against the Romans.

Also the revolutionary tradition of first century Judaism had its antecedents in the Old Testament, for instance, in 1 Sam. 15:1-3, which advocates the annihilation of the Amalekites in the name and at the command of God, and considers Israel's enemies to be God's enemies. The tradition of a holy war re-emerged at the time of the Maccabees who liberated Israel from the Syrian oppressor (1 Macc. 2:15-20). The ideals of the

9. Benedictions 10 and 12 of Shemoneh Esreh.

Maccabean liberation remained alive even though the Maccabean state quickly degenerated into oriental despotism.

About the time of Jesus' boyhood, the Zealotic movement appeared as a political underground organization.[10] Their zeal was not exhausted in the struggle for liberation from Rome, but it had an essentially eschatological orientation, namely, the realization of God's sovereign reign by means of a holy war. Radical faith in God and political subversion, kidnappings, hit and run guerrilla tactics form a unity of commitment for the sake of the kingdom of God. If God is to be king in the Holy Land, then loyalty toward the pagan emperor and payment of taxes are treason against God and the first commandment. God's sovereignty in Israel demands liberation from Caesar. Programs of social justice must be enacted, debtors be released, the land redistributed, and slaves freed. Hence, when the Zealots gained the upper hand in Jerusalem in A.D. 66, they burned the city archives, the land registers, and the accounts of debt.

It was self-evident to the Zealots that the Roman government constituted not an institution of God but of Satan and his kin. The Zealotic idea of theocracy was incompatible with the attitude of political loyalty. Yet what the Zealots actually accomplished was not the establishment of the kingdom of God, but the destruction of Jerusalem by Rome in A.D. 70.

United with the Zealots in their hatred against Rome were the Apocalypticists who believed that the present evil age is under the dominion of demonic powers manifested in the empires of this world.[11] World history constitutes a process of progressive degeneration which finds its culmination in an empire of Satanic proportion. The fate of the righteous in this age, therefore, is persecution and suffering. But comes the time appointed by God, then God himself, or a heavenly Son of man, will overthrow the empires of the world in cataclysmic up-

10. M. Hengel, *Die Zeloten. Untersuchungen zur Jüdischen Freiheitsbewegung in der Zeit von Herodes 1 bis 70 n. Chr.* (Leiden: Brill, 1961); *Victory over Violence. Jesus and the Revolutionists* (Philadelphia: Fortress Press, 1973).

11. D. S. Russell, *The Method and Message of Jewish Apocalyptic, 200 B.C.– 100* (Philadelphia: Westminster Press, 1964).

heavals, destroy all sinners, and vindicate his elect. The primary interests of apocalyptic theology consist in speculation about the divisions of world history, the apocalyptic timetable and the great cosmic transformation of all things at the End. The End in some way will correspond to the Beginning (e.g., 2 Esd. 6:1–6; 7:30; 2 Bar. 3:7), but only occasionally does apocalypticism speak about the nature of God's eschatological reign. As a matter of fact, the phrase "the kingdom of God" or "of heaven" is found only a few times in this type of literature because its focus lies in the final judgment and the overthrow of demonic powers and empires, rather than in God's eschatological reign.

It would appear obvious that the dualism of the two ages prevented a positive relationship to Caesar's empire in principle. Moreover, since the cataclysmic transformation at the End could also be thought to result in the glorification of the national theocracy, therefore, apocalypticism could also interact with the nationalistic hope and add fuel to the fire which the Zealots tried to spark.

The Qumran community[12] combined the apocalyptic dualism of two ages with a doctrine of two realms which are determined by two spirits created by God. The spirit of falsehood rules over the children of darkness (1 QS 3:15). The spirit of truth determines the children of light who had withdrawn from the world into the desert of Qumran in order to establish the true theocracy. They are commanded "to hate all children of darkness" (1 QS 1:3–4). And at the time appointed by God they will defeat the children of darkness in a war to end all wars and establish the theocracy in glory. In the meantime, the "mini-theocracy" of Qumran guarded its separation from the realm of darkness and maintained a posture of political quietism toward Caesar's world outside.

We have seen that at Jesus' time divergent approaches to the problem of the relation of God's kingdom to Caesar's kingdom prevailed in Judaism. To some Jews, God's reign in Israel

12. G. Vermes, *The Dead Sea Scrolls in English,* a Pelican book (New York: Penguin Books, 1962). H. Ringgren, *The Faith of Qumran* (Philadelphia: Fortress Press, 1963).

existed within Caesar's reign and Caesar's reign existed within the reign of God, who, as king of the world, had established Caesar's kingdom as his ordinance. Hence, a penultimate loyalty toward Caesar was demanded so long as Caesar did not encroach upon the reign of God in Israel. But to others, the mere presence of the idolatrous empire of Caesar was an encroachment upon Yahweh's reign in Israel. Hence, they either took a posture of political quietism in the present, hoping for a national or an apocalyptic reversal through a Messiah or through God himself, or else they actively called for revolution in the present as anticipation and initiation of the eschatological kingdom of God.

A common bond which united these diverse attitudes was that God's reign in Israel is and shall be a theocracy, and the theocracy has a Torah structure. Though diminished in size and thrust into a position of being vassals to Rome, the Jews who were faithful to the Torah believed that the God who had chosen them reigned over them through his law which was his full revelation for all aspects of life. Even if the scope of the authority of the Jewish government in Jerusalem had been severely curtailed, the theocracy still functioned. Naturally, there were also those Jews who could not have cared less about any of this, whose struggle to make a living or whose opportunism prompted them to see in Caesar's kingdom the only kingdom there was.

Jesus and the Kingdom of God

When Jesus announced, "the kingdom of God is at hand" (Mark 1:15), he was not speaking of a theocratic state on earth within or against Caesar's empire, but of God's eschatological reign which the turn of the ages would bring.

Jesus separated the kingdom of God from Israel's national expectations of glory and victory over her oppressors. He was as much opposed to the political messianism and revolutionary Zealotism of his day[13] as he was removed from speculations

13. M. Hengel, *Was Jesus a Revolutionist?* Facet Books, Biblical Series (Philadelphia: Fortress Press, 1971).

about apocalyptic timetables concerning the End. But, in agreement with Jewish Apocalypticists, he believed that the decisive turn of the ages, when sin, sickness, poverty, demons, and death would be no more, will be brought about by God alone and not by man's cooperation, least of all by man's work of violence and bloodshed. A person's proper response in the face of the coming kingdom of God consists in repentance, which does not mean "crying over spilt milk," or feeling sorry that one has not become "religious" sooner, but which involves a total turning toward God and a radical reorientation of one's whole being.

Jesus' call to repentance, unlike John the Baptist's, was not based upon the impending wrath of God. Not that Jesus rejected the doctrine of a final judgment as though it were an antiquated idea. For him the coming reign of God is first and foremost "good news," evoking joy and joyful surprise (Matt. 13:44–46). His call to repentance also implies: Don't miss the hour, but accept God's offer of salvation (Luke 14:15, 24). His kingdom appears "automatically," "by itself" (Mark 14:28). Like the fruit of the earth, it comes as a miracle wrought by God without man's cooperation. Neither the heeding of the Pharisaic slogan: "Take the yoke of the kingdom upon you," nor the realization of Zealotic programs will usher in the kingdom of God. But if his eschatological reign consists in a miracle, then how, when, and where does it come?

To questions like these, Jesus gave seemingly contradictory answers. On one hand we hear that the reign of God lies in the future; on the other hand we are told that it is in some way already present. This tension alone would seem to indicate that the eschatological reign of God is not an event in history to which we can assign a definite date, nor did it come prior to Jesus. It would be meaningless to say of an historical event that it is both present and future. For Jesus, the kingdom of God is God's saving power which will end history and which casts its effects and its light into the present in and through his own ministry.

The future coming of the kingdom is clearly expressed in the parables of the sower, the mustard seed, the leaven, and in sayings about "entering the kingdom of heaven." These parables do not speak of the kingdom in terms of an evolutionary process in history. Their point is not the progress of Christianity from small beginnings in Galilee to the Christian empire of Constantine, or the church universal, or to the Christian century. The point of these parables is the joyful surprise at the End, and its miraculous results.

How soon will the End come? It does not come with signs to indicate how far away it still is. Rather, suddenly and unexpectedly it will be among you (Luke 17:20 ff.). Jesus set no time limit on the appearance of the kingdom, nor did he give one definite apocalyptic form to his proclamation of the future reign of God, but instead spoke in parables about it. Through them the future reign becomes transparent and impinges upon the present. The linear time-line between the now and the End becomes a matter of secondary importance when man's present existence is already determined by God's future.

The signs of the kingdom are present for those who have eyes to see. "If it is by the finger of God that I cast out demons, then the kingdom of God has come upon you" (Luke 11:20). If in Jesus' exorcisms the future kingdom of God is already experienced in terms of conflict with and victory over demonic powers, then it is experienced in the other healing miracles as fulfillment of Isaiah's promise (Matt. 11:5; Isa. 35:5) and as gracious gift of a new life. Hence, "Blessed are the eyes which see what you see! For I tell you that many prophets and kings desired to see what you see, and did not see it" (Luke 10:23–24). In Jesus' ministry the eschatological kingdom is present as power that heals and saves by grace alone.

Yet the kingdom is present in Jesus' ministry only in terms of conflict, ambiguity, and hiddenness. Also the healed persons died and Jesus was rejected by some in spite of (according to John 11, because of) his miracles (Mark 3:22; Luke 11:15 par.). But the presence of the kingdom in Jesus' healing ministry could also be experienced as a foretaste of an unambiguous future. To his followers Jesus' ministry of healing was not meant to be the End but the Beginning, or rather, the inbreaking of the End in a new Beginning.

The same applies to his ministry of the word. The parables of the lost sheep, the lost coin, and the prodigal son (Luke 15) speak about the nature of God's eschatological reign breaking into the present. The structure of the kingdom is not the Torah, but God's undeserved grace toward sinful man. The kingdom is merited not as compensation for pious works performed, but it is received as gift of grace or it is not received at all. Hence, "whoever does not receive the kingdom of God like a child shall not enter it" (Mark 10:15).

Because the structure of the kingdom is not the Torah but grace and forgiveness, Jesus turned to the "lost sheep out of the house of Israel," forgave sins in the place of God, and had fellowship with "publicans and sinners," celebrating the saving reign of God with people who, by the standards of the Torah, were excluded from it (Matt. 15:24; 11:19; Mark 2:5). He transcended the boundaries of Israel's theocracy when he promised that "many will come from the East and the West and sit with Abraham, Isaac, and Jacob in the kingdom of heaven" (Matt. 8:11). In the light of God's coming reign the Torah-enforced distinctions between Jew and gentile, clean and unclean food, leper and healthy, righteous and unrighteous, publican and Zealot are relativized and robbed of their determinative power. What matters now is repentance, that is, being open to God's reign present already in Jesus' ministry and simultaneously yet to come.

Because Jesus was not merely the proclaimer of the kingdom but also the representative and bearer of the kingdom, he called men to follow him, forgave sins, thus placing his authority over that of Moses. Conversely, doing business as usual, trusting in one's accumulated wealth, barricading oneself behind traditions, denouncing the presence of the kingdom in Jesus' ministry as manifestations of demonic power mean to invite the eschatological judgment which will also express the victory of the King over his rebels (Luke 6:24; Mark 7:1–23; 3:22; Matt. 13:30).

The Governance of God

It needs to be emphasized today that not everything Jesus had to say about God had an eschatological thrust. To put it differently, one must distinguish his eschatological proclamation of the future coming of the kingdom from God's present governance of this world.

This distinction has its antecedents in the Bible of Jesus, the Old Testament. While Second and Third Isaiah promised the appearance of God's reign at the end of time, we find that the enthronement psalms (Psalms 47; 93; 96; 97) speak of God's reign as an accomplished fact and not as hope for the future. "Yahweh reigns," "Yahweh has become king" is the confession in which his kingship was celebrated in Israel during the annual enthronement festivals.

Jesus generally reserved the terminology of kingship for his eschatological proclamation of God's future reign, the exception being Matt. 5:35. Yet he also spoke of God's noneschatological rule in the present as Creator, Preserver, and Lawgiver. All of this we seek to express with the term "governance."

Jesus declared that God "makes his sun rise on the evil and on the good, and sends rain on the just and the unjust" (Matt. 5:45). In agreement with Judaism Jesus affirmed God's governance over nature (cf. Jer. 14:22). The world appears here not from the perspective of eschatology as hastening to its doom. It appears rather as the realm of God's providential care and governance. Over against a radical apocalyptic or gnostic dualism, Jesus affirmed that God has not surrendered his creation to Satan, but preserves it and takes care of it in such a way that no sparrow "will fall to the ground without your Father's will" (Matt. 10:29).

God's governance also includes the protection of life, marriage, and the family through the law of Moses. The prohibitions of the Decalogue presuppose the presence of sin within man and seek to curb its effects. The Mosaic divorce laws were given against "your hardness of heart" (Mark 10:5), "as judgment on the people."[14]

The commandments in general are measures to dam sin's unbridled torrent and to regulate life in community. Therefore, Jesus can speak without sarcasm of good and evil persons, righteous and unrighteous (Luke 5:32; Matt. 5:39). He did not disagree with the rich young man who asserted that he had kept commandments five through eight (Mark 10:19–20), and the Pharisee who thanked God in the temple that he was not an extortioner or an unjust man, etc., was not corrected for making false claims. These men were righteous as far as individual commandments were concerned through which God protects life and regulates interpersonal relationships.

Even people who are "evil" in God's sight can "give good gifts to [their] children" (Matt. 7:11). Also those who do not heed the call to repentance and do not receive the kingdom of God as a child stand under the demands of God's governance and can perform works of justice. Jesus' saying that only a good tree bears good fruit (Matt. 7:16–20) may not be interpreted to mean that only his disciples can perform works of civil righteousness. Hence, Jesus calls the Pharisees righteous even though they did not follow him.

The realm of God's governance also includes the Roman Empire; otherwise Jesus would not have enjoined the people to pay taxes to Caesar (Mark 12:17). "The kings of the Gentiles exercise lordship over them; and those in authority over them are called benefactors. . . . But I am among you as one who serves" (Luke 22:25–27).

Two distinct kinds of rule are contrasted here. On the one hand Jesus speaks of Caesar's power politics. As enforcer of law and order, of peace and justice, Caesar wants to appear as a

14. E. Schweizer, *The Good News According to Mark,* ed. D. H. Madvig (Richmond: John Knox Press, 1970), p. 203. Concerning the methodology of working from the written Gospels via sources and oral traditions back to "the historical Jesus," see N. Perrin, *Rediscovering the Teachings of Jesus* (New York: Harper, 1967) and John Reumann, *Jesus in the Church's Gospels. Modern Scholarship and the Earliest Sources* (Philadelphia: Fortress Press, 1968).

"benefactor." On the other hand there is Jesus the servant, whose rule consists in the renunciation of power to enforce God's will and whose rule manifests that love which bears all things to the bitter end. The two rules must be distinguished from each other in kind as well as in duration. Caesar's reign pertains to this age only. Christ's servanthood manifests the eschaton in the present as loving service that saves sinners.

Yet we may not ignore that both rules are under God. Jesus did not in principle equate Caesar's power politics with the kingdom of Satan as the Zealots did. It rather stands under the lordship of that God who raises empires and smashes them again and who desires that Caesars should indeed be "benefactors," using power for the welfare of their people, restraining the destructiveness of sin and evil, and advancing justice.

While Jesus did not demonize Caesar's power politics, neither did he simply equate Caesar's laws with God's will, much less did he assign an autonomous sphere to earthly rulers. Because God rules some of the temporal affairs of his creatures through Caesar's power politics, therefore Jesus, in stark contrast to the Zealots, demanded the payment of taxes as a rightful obligation and he upheld the extremely limited scope in which first century Jews participated in the empire—a scope limited to paying taxes and being impressed into temporary governmental service (Matt. 7:41; e.g., Mark 15:21).

However, the emphasis of Mark 12:17 lies on the second part: "*but* [render] unto God that which belongs to God," namely, your whole self. Thus the mythology of the empire with which the Caesars adorned their politics is herewith set aside as pagan junk. Set aside also is the Zealotic hatred of the empire which revealed merely self-righteous hearts.

Simultaneously, surrender to God automatically limits obedience to Caesar and in case of conflict between God's will and Caesar's decrees, the saying of Matt. 6:24 is normative: one cannot serve two masters. Hence, "what belongs to Caesar" is to be determined ever anew, for Caesar's changing laws are not identical with the will of God, but they need not be opposed to it in principle. Finally, what belongs to Caesar will ultimately perish together with Caesar when God's eschatological kingdom appears in glory.

In conclusion: (1) Jesus neither withdrew from the world and "its evil generation" into the purity of the desert in order to play religion there, nor did he establish a theocratic counter kingdom against Caesar's in the Holy Land.

(2) He accepted Caesar's kingdom as part of God's governance of this world, and he accepted the law of Moses as God's law which restrains the destructiveness of sin and as rule which regulates life in community. But he expected man's salvation to come neither from Moses' law, although it was given by God, nor even less from Caesar's decrees, but from God's eschatological reign alone. As we shall see in the next chapter Jesus distinguished between God's will and Moses' law, and this distinction would of course be even more applicable for Caesar's law.

(3) The kingdom of God is not a Torah-structured ideal society on earth, nor does it consist in rules to be enforced, but it appears as God's eschatological love embracing those who have broken God's law. Yet the eschaton also consists in God's judgment upon all unwilling to live in this love, and in both ways it reveals who God is and what man is. Until then the two imperatives apply to all: "Render to Caesar the things that are Caesar's" and "Repent, for the kingdom of God is at hand."

"YOU HAVE HEARD THAT IT WAS SAID TO THE MEN OF OLD. . . . BUT I SAY TO YOU . . ."

In the theocracy the law of God is simultaneously the national law. Obedience to it assures God's favor and blessing. The pious did not find the law to be a burden. On the contrary, to them it was a delight (cf. Psalm 1). For Jesus the themes of Israel's election and of the covenant receded into the background and were not developed by him. In the forefront of his proclamation we find the themes of the eschatological kingdom of God and of the will of God. The question arises: How is the will of God related to the Moses Torah and to the kingdom of God?

The Ethical Teaching of Jesus

Jesus' attitude toward the Torah seems to be contradictory at first glance since we find affirmation and criticism of the Torah side by side. For instance, when the young man asked what he must do to inherit eternal life, Jesus referred him to the law (Mark 10:17). He sent the cleansed leper to the priest to offer the prescribed sacrifice for his purification (Mark 1:44). He answered the scribe's question concerning the first commandment by quoting Deut. 6:4 and Lev. 19:18 (Mark 12:29–33).

Nor did Jesus object in principle to the "oral law" which in rabbinic Judaism was an integral part of the Torah. He even wore the traditional clothing of the pious and attended the synagogue, a postexilic institution. In short, he accepted customs which had not been founded upon the written law, but which belonged to the "tradition of the fathers."

Yet on occasion Jesus critically distinguished between the will of God and the oral law: "So, for the sake of your tradition, you have made void the word of God" (Matt. 15:6). In matters of fasting and sabbath observance Jesus was "a liberal." From the viewpoint of the pious there was no reason why he should not have waited until sundown on the sabbath to heal people who had been ill, some even for decades. He could have prayed with them until sundown and then healed them instead of offending the Pharisees. Above all, there was no need to tell a healed person to carry his pallet on the sabbath or have his disciples pluck ears of corn on the sabbath (Mark 2:23–27; 3:1–5; Luke 13:11–17; 14:1–5; John 5:1–9). Such incidents indicated to many that Jesus lacked proper respect for the law, and since he proclaimed the kingdom of God, such disrespect was all the more scandalous.

Jesus viewed the matter differently: "The sabbath was made for man, not man for the sabbath" (Mark 2:27). No rabbi would have agreed with this position. But he went even further and also critized the written law itself by stating that a man does not become clean through rites of purification and he does not become impure from eating food which is not kosher (Mark 7:14–21). When the distinction between ritual purity and impurity is dissolved then the authority of the written law is no longer absolute. Hence, Jesus had table fellowship with tax collectors and sinners whose purity was nil in the sight of the Torah. Jesus exhibited a freedom over against the law which no pious Jew, no rabbi or prophet, could afford and which gave rise to the charge that he was a false prophet.

He also distinguished between the Mosaic divorce legislation and the Creator's original will (Mark 10:1-9), and on his own authority he radicalized the Decalogue, introducing his teaching with: "But *I* say unto you." To be sure, he rejected out of hand neither the law nor the prophets of the Old Testament, but he did not simply equate them with the will of God either. He liberated the will of God from legalism and literalism so that no one could be comfortable behind a screen of rules and avoid the all-piercing will of God who does not tolerate hatred, or sinful desires, not even legal divorce, not even legal recourse for injuries received (Luke 6:27-30; Matt. 5:22, 28, 32, 34, 39).

The proclaimer of the kingdom of God revealed the will of God with finality. He intensified the prohibitions of the Decalogue to the utmost and reduced the whole of the law to the twofold commandments of love toward God and toward the neighbor (Mark 12:28-31). But Jesus also extended the term neighbor to everybody, including one's enemy (Matt. 5:44) and insisted that love which does not include the enemy is mere self-gratification. The fatherhood of God demands the brotherhood of man, including the enemy.[15] Fantastically simple, but it is scandalous when you think of its implications.

The Father who does not carry out his vengeance upon the evil but accepts his prodigals in mercy and offers his home to the righteous, challenges Zealots and tax collectors alike to be peacemakers. The poor are not to revenge themselves upon the rich nor the persecuted upon their oppressors. Their behavior of love is the fruit of God's deed which liberates from hatred. The rich who are warned against the idolatry of depending on their

15. For the Old Testament see: Lev. 19:34; Exod. 23:4; Prov. 25:21. Hatred of God's enemies was commanded in Qumran, 1. QS1:3-4, nurtured in apocalyptic and Zealotic piety and expressed in Old Testament psalms of revenge, e.g., Ps. 109:6-13.

possessions are challenged to see their brothers in the poor (Luke 6:24; Mark 10:25; Luke 19:8; 10:30–37).

Yet we must also take into account that Jesus abolished the basic principle of Israel's penal law, the law of retribution:[16] "An eye for an eye and a tooth for a tooth" (Matt. 5:38–39). This principle was meant to curb man's desire for unbridled revenge and simultaneously to assure that God's commandments would not be transgressed with impunity. The punishment meted out should correspond to the transgression. Without the principle of retribution—however it may be applied—any law, anywhere becomes a farce. But Jesus abolished it with one stroke. "Don't resist one who is evil." If anyone sues you, don't stand on your legal rights but give more than is demanded of you. Love sets aside even the retribution demanded by God's law, just as it sets aside the legal divorce permitted by Moses or the "natural" reaction toward one's enemy.

To be sure, the injunctions in Matt. 5:29 and 40 are hyperboles and not meant to be taken literally; otherwise Jesus' hearers would have become cripples and been arrested for indecent exposure. But they are illustrations of the radical nature of God's will, which tolerates no hypocrisy or self-centeredness, no matter how cleverly veiled.

Of course, we at once would raise objections and ask how all of this translates into operative principles for individuals in ecclesiastical and political life today. What would happen to my inalienable rights, not to speak of the national welfare, if the demanding will of God as taught by Jesus were to become normative? Sociologists might even point out that in the "simple setting of first century rural Palestine" such demands were appropriate, but in our complex twentieth century society they are no longer relevant. This objection misses the point because the demands of the will of God were as shocking to the hearers of Jesus as they are today—perhaps even more so since they had been brought up with the presupposition that the Moses Torah was identical with the will of God.

The real question is: Does such radical love really express

16. Exod. 21:24; Lev. 24:20; Deut. 19:21.

God's will? Is what Jesus said true, that God cannot be satisfied with divided loyalty and partial commitment to him and to our fellow men? What does it mean: "Thy will be done on earth as it is in heaven," except that the radical love that breaks through every boundary is to find expression in our words and in our actions? The God who "makes his sun rise on the evil and on the good and sends rain on the just and the unjust" draws no lines between our friends and our foes. He is not on the side of our national aspirations and does not identify with our causes. Instead of demonizing our enemies, personal or national, the pure will of God demands love of the enemy and renunciation of self-love.

This kind of love is the essence of the freedom of the sons and daughters of the Father in heaven to which Jesus calls his disciples (Matt. 5:45). The "as yourself" in the commandment to love the neighbor does not command self-love, but provides the criterion for the love of neighbor and requires renunciation of self (Luke 14:26).

What we do or do not do for the neighbor is of ultimate significance in the final judgment because the Lord identifies with the poor and the hungry, the sick and those who despair of life (Matt. 25:31–46). Several aspects of this parable are striking. First, what the "blessed" have done is what anyone could do. Second, their actions toward the hungry are done for the sake of the hungry alone, not for the sake of God, nor with side glances at eternal rewards to come. Third, the cursed want to make their ignorance about God's identification with the poor into an excuse for their neglect. If they had been certain that in meeting the downtrodden they were meeting the Lord himself, then they would not have "walked by on the other side" (cf. Luke 10:30–37).

The provocativeness of the parable of the good Samaritan which stung the first audience becomes apparent to us if we substitute atheist for the Samaritan; Lutheran bishop and pastor for the priest and Levite; Jew, Black, or Indian for the man who fell among thieves. Whole churches have managed to sing the Gloria and pray the Lord's Prayer—"Thy will be done on earth"—and then, leaving their Jerusalem, walked by the miserable making excuses.

In short, Jesus, instead of enforcing a multitude of rules, prohibitions, and interpretations, called his hearers back to the central demand of love toward God and the neighbor, radicalizing and extending this demand so that no sphere of life is excluded. He also called them back to God's originial will in creation (Matt. 19:8, 6, 9) in contrast to the Moses Torah.

Finally he summoned his disciples to a behavior which appeared scandalous in the light of the fourth commandment. This is all the more remarkable since he defended the fourth commandment against scribal casuistry (Matt. 15:3–6). But to the disciple who wished to first bury his father—which was an absolute obligation to a first century Jew—he replied: "Follow me, and leave the dead to bury their own dead" (Matt. 8:22). This is probably the most scandalous saying of Jesus. In the same vein we hear: "If any one comes to me and does not hate his own father and mother and wife and children and brothers and sisters, yes, and even his own life, he cannot be my disciple" (Luke 14:26). Of course, this is hyperbolic language and hatred here is not an expression of egocentricity but of renunciation of that which one holds dearest.

The point is that discipleship is to be the fulfillment of the first commandment, total commitment to God and his will, "to fear love and trust in God above all things," so that natural loyalties, protected by the fourth commandment, are relativized and abrogated.

Typical Interpretations of Jesus' Ethical Teaching

Before we deal further with this subject, we shall take a glance at some interpretations of Jesus' radical teaching concerning God's will.

Pre-Vatican II Catholicism distinguishes between two classes of people and two types of demands. The ethical teachings of Jesus were labeled "evangelical counsels" for spiritual athletes who sought to be perfect, like members of monasteries. Ordinary Christians are directed to the law of Moses as the minimum requirement. The strength of this approach lies in its realism; its weakness is that the differentiation between two classes of disciples is unknown in the New Testament.

The traditional Lutheran interpretation held that Jesus' ethical teaching applies to all men and convicts all men of their sinfulness and thus seeks to lead them to repentance. When we hear the demands of the Sermon on the Mount, we can hardly say, "All these things have I observed from my youth" (Mark 10:20). What adultery and murder are we may know from hearsay. Both are certainly avoidable. But when I understand what Jesus meant by hatred or by sinful desires (Matt. 5:22, 28), I understand such feelings only because they are not foreign to me. I know them, not from hearsay, but because I myself have hated or lusted. In that case the demands of Jesus indeed condemn us because they find us to be sinners already.

The strength of the traditional Lutheran approach lies in its realism and its universalism. Its weakness is that neither for Jesus nor for Matthew is the sole purpose of the ethical teaching to be found in convicting us of our sins. The Sermon on the Mount demands the practice of love by those who have repented.

Some Protestants argued that what Jesus really wanted with his ethical teaching was not concrete actions but the right disposition and motivation. However, the New Testament insists that love has to find concrete expression in action and that hate is already an action of the heart.

Albert Schweitzer held that Jesus' expectation of the imminent End and the imminent coming of the kingdom of God conditioned his ethical teaching. His radical demands were appropriate only for the short interval between Jesus' appearance and the impending doomsday. Even as in situations of great national crises emergency decrees are issued which would be inappropriate for ordinary times, so Jesus called for special "heroic" efforts in the face of the final crisis which he thought would come in the immediate future. His ethics is "interim ethics," not "kingdom ethics," and it is determined by the expectation of the imminent End. Since Jesus' eschatological hopes turned out to be mistaken, therefore his ethical radicalism is no longer relevant.

In this exposition the insight is correct that the demands of Jesus are not intended for the future kingdom because then hatred, poverty, and marriage will be no more, but the demands do apply to the interim before the End. However, Schweitzer not only ignored the presence of the kingdom in Jesus' ministry in the form of radical love which embraces even unheroic creatures like publicans, but above all, he did not see that the content of Jesus' ethical demands is never based upon the eschatological hope in general,[17] or the expectation of the imminent End in particular. For instance, the demand "love your enemies" is issued not because doomsday or the kingdom is around the corner and hence old grudges should be buried, but it is based upon the governance of God who daily lets his sun rise on the evil and the good. To take another example, the prohibition of divorce is grounded in the will of the Creator from the beginning (Mark 10:5).

In short, Jesus' ethical teaching is determined by his awareness of the eternal will of God and not by his expectation of the imminent End. The expectation of the coming kingdom produced the eschatological demand "repent," turn to God. However, this expectation did not give content to the ethical demands. Also in this interim between Jesus' appearance and the End God's will is not different from what it has always been.

The perfectionistic interpretation sees in Jesus a new lawgiver and argues that obedience to his new law is the condition for entering the kingdom of God.

It is true that Jesus expected his disciples to manifest in their action that love which expresses the will of God. Indeed, God renders judgment on the last day according to our works of love, done or undone (Matt. 6:14–15; 25:40). The demand "be merciful ["perfect" in Matt. 5:48], even as your Father is merciful" (Luke 6:36) applies to all disciples.

However, the perfectionistic interpretation ignores that the ground of Jesus' demand is the unconditional offer of salvation expressed, for instance, in the Beatitudes (Matt. 5:3–9), in the

17. This error is repeated in J. T. Sanders, *Ethics in the New Testament* (Philadelphia: Fortress Press, 1975), pp. 1–29.

parables of the lost (Luke 15), in Jesus' healings, or in his fellowship with tax collectors and sinners.

What then is the relationship between the offer of salvation and the radical demand of the will of God? Through the mercy of the father, the prodigal son is received; even before he can ask for forgiveness, the father embraces him. But, as son, he cannot continue in "loose living" (Luke 15:13). Through Jesus the disciples are drawn into the gravitational pull of the kingdom of God and of the merciful father so that his mercy and his will become effective in them and through them. If, however, forgiveness received does not become forgiveness granted to the fellow man including the enemy, then condemnation is God's final word (Matt. 18:23–35). Finally, it should be noted that the picture of Jesus' followers as presented by the evangelists is the picture not of perfect saints, but of misunderstanding persons and of men of little faith who are struggling along the way.

Christian utopianism regarded the Sermon on the Mount as Christ's political program for establishing a new society of love and peace. Hence, utopians advocated the abolition of armed forces, of the police, and the whole judicial system of the state in the name of Matt. 5:39, "Do not resist one who is evil." The law of love was to be translated into all aspects of social-political life. (Of course, when it comes to Jesus' prohibition of divorce, many a modern utopian squirms. Love of the enemy might have its place in politics, but not in marriage. Fascinating!)

This approach ignores that the kingdom of God is not a sociological entity and is not established through man's moral action. Furthermore, obedience to the demands of the Sermon on the Mount presupposes repentance, discipleship, a new heart. These presuppositions are lacking in any pluralistic society just as they were absent within Judaism of Jesus' day. Without them Matt. 5:39 would lead to anarchy.

The Law of Moses, the Law of Caesar, and the Demands of Jesus

We have seen that Jesus broke the unity which, for Judaism, existed between the Moses Torah and the will of God, even as he dissolved the identity between the national theocracy and the people of God. The kingdom of God will not be a restored theocracy with the Moses Torah as the law of the land. Therefore, the difference between the pagan empire of Rome and the national Jewish theocracy is no longer absolute, but relative. However, Jesus accepted the Moses Torah also as a means of regulating interpersonal existence in a preliminary way, even as he accepted the law of the Roman emperor demanding taxes.

Let us take a closer look. The question, "Is it lawful to pay taxes to Caesar, or not?" (Mark 12:14), is a question oriented to the Torah. To what extent are members of the theocracy in which the Torah constitutes the law of the nation obligated toward Caesar? Jesus ignored that legalistic question because for him salvation is not Torah-structured. A parallel to this approach is found when he liberated the question, "Who is my neighbor?" from the context of the Torah. Is it a person obedient to the Torah, any Jew, a good foreigner, or who? Jesus ignored the Torah orientation and demanded love also toward the enemy.

On what basis did Jesus demand payment of taxes to Caesar or love toward one's enemy? In the first instance he made it clear that the person who renders unto God the things which are God's is obligated to Caesar in a penultimate way. That person is already drawn into the gravitational pull of God's kingdom which relativizes the distinction between the Jewish theocracy and the pagan empire, because God's eschatological reign has a non-Torah structure. Simultaneously the person who surrenders to God lives in the world over which Caesar rules for the time being.

In the second instance, Jesus based the demand to love the enemy not on the Torah, but on the goodness of the Creator and Preserver toward the righteous and the unrighteous. The goodness of the Creator and Preserver relativizes the Torah-oriented distinction between members of the theocracy and gentiles, between the righteous and the unrighteous, and this goodness is present in Jesus who calls sinners.

How can one then discover the obligation toward Caesar or toward the neighbor? The coin bears Caesar's image. This discloses God's will that—for the time being—Caesar rules the land and one owes him certain things, such as taxes. The concrete demand of God meets us in concrete situations and can be discovered by those who have surrendered to God himself. Love toward the neighbor is to be shown where God places us, as neighbor, before one who needs our help (Luke 10:29–37).

It should have become obvious by now why Jesus projected no social-political programs for reshaping the world. What love demands in concrete situations cannot be legislated in advance. It can only be discovered ever anew. The good Samaritan did not apply rules which he had memorized, but he discovered step by step what needed to be done.

Furthermore, the radical demand of love enunciated by Jesus cannot serve as norm for our social legislation. It presupposes and continually aims at the profession of discipleship, the new heart, and repentance, while social legislation must deal realistically not with eternal salvation but with earthly preservation and justice which can be *enforced* by the proper use of power. Christ, however, forces no man to accept God's mercy and live by it. A "Christian" empire, small or large, in the desert or the city, with its own power structure was exactly what Jesus did not wish to establish, according to the temptation narrative (Matthew 4). He did not even issue a program for the general redistribution of wealth.

Of course, his call for freedom from dependence on riches has direct social implications whenever disciples are numerically noticeable in a community. The same applies to his demand to express concretely love toward God and the neighbor in situations of everyday life. The love demanded by Jesus will, of necessity, always point beyond the social status quo. It represents the discomfort and disquiet within the social structures of this world, and disciples, instead of upholding the unjust status quo, must seek to change social conditions which hurt neighbors and class enemies. The love exhibited by the good Samaritan was not blind, but it discovered what was necessary in that particular situation.

The ethical teaching of Jesus is understood by the first evangelist to be the eschatological fulfillment of the Moses Torah (5:17). Nevertheless, Matthew insists that the Torah of Moses has validity "till heaven and earth pass away" (5:18). This does not mean forever and ever, but means until the End. Apart from the eschatological fulfillment of the law by Jesus, apart from repentance and discipleship of those who are drawn into the kingdom already now, the law which permits divorce and the law which demands retribution have validity until the End. The world can no more exist without the principle of retribution than it can exist without divorce legislation. It needs laws to restrain the power of sin.

Jesus' ethical teaching is neither a supplement to the Torah nor a substitute for laws which regulate life in society. They are rather paradigms which indicate "the fruit of repentance" (Matt. 3:8) of those whose hardness of heart has been overcome by God's eschatological deed in Jesus' ministry. Until the eschaton the disciple also stands under the law of the governmental authority, which at Jesus' time was represented by the emperor Tiberius and his prefect in Judea, Pontius Pilate.

Crucified under Pontius Pilate

Even though it is absurd to argue that Jesus was a revolutionist in league with the Zealots,[18] nevertheless the radicalism of Jesus' demand and his proclamation of a non-Torah–structured kingdom made him suspect with the authorities of the theocracy, the Sadducees. Jesus, like the Zealots, called for radical commitment to God, ignoring or rejecting prudent behavior as the best way to get along. He, like they, spoke of the coming kingdom of God and both, for different reasons, viewed the status quo with critical eyes. Jesus' preaching reached to the heart of the theocracy, the Torah. A Sadducean perspective would wish a plague on both of them, since they endangered the status quo which the Sadducees were bent on upholding.

To Zealots, Jesus probably appeared as a political quietist, a Jewish "Uncle Tom" who lacked the sense or the courage to

18. Cf. note 13.

fight the pagan oppressor. Moreover, he commited the unpardonable sin of requesting the payment of taxes to the pagan enemy of the reign of God. The Pharisees were offended because his teaching displaced the Torah-oriented distinction between righteous and sinners. To the Sadducees, Jesus was a threat not only because he had a following, but also because they understood that if his cause should prevail, the theocracy would be in peril.

Whatever role Jerusalem's Sanhedrin played or, rather, did not play, it would be fair to say that the representatives of the theocracy in the persons of Annas and Caiaphas rejected Jesus and his claim concerning the kingdom of God and the will of God. The form which this rejection took is unknown to us.[19]

At any rate, it was before Caesar's representative that Jesus appeared at trial, and it was this Roman, Pontius Pilate, who condemned him to death by crucifixion. Had Pilate merely confirmed the verdict of a Jewish court, Jesus would have been executed by stoning, the punishment prescribed by the Torah for false prophets. The fact of Jesus' crucifixion demonstrates that Pilate treated him as a political criminal, a revolutionist, on the same level with Barabbas, "who had committed murder in the insurrection" (Mark 15:7). One can only conjecture how much Pilate actually knew about Jesus, or whether Pilate, in good faith, that is, in total ignorance of the facts concerning Jesus, passed judgment on him, or, what seems more likely, whether he was persuaded by some influential Sadducees like Annas and Caiaphas to eliminate Jesus as a threat to the status quo.

To the disciples, however, the crucifixion of Jesus meant more than merely another act of miscarried Roman justice. It meant that the representative of the kingdom of God had been rejected by the representatives of the theocracy and of the empire. According to the Torah: "Cursed by God is he who hangs on a tree."

In conclusion: (1) Just as the kingdom of God is not a

19. Caiaphas' tenure as high-priest lasted longest in the century prior to A.D. 70, which would indicate that Pilate and he got along well. His father-in-law, Annas, a powerful schemer, managed that his own five sons eventually became high-priests. On the problems of the trial of Jesus, see G. S. Sloyan, *Jesus on Trial* (Philadelphia: Fortress Press, 1973).

counter-empire against Caesar, so the radical demands of Jesus to love and discipleship do not once and for all displace that law which demands retribution against transgressors.

(2) The demands of Jesus fulfill the law eschatologically and function as permanent disquiet within this world.

(3) This disquiet was experienced by representatives of the theocracy and of the empire in that they reacted with violence toward him who represented the kingdom of God and the will of God.

"CHRIST HAS LIBERATED US FROM THE CURSE OF THE LAW" AND "LET EVERY PERSON BE SUBJECT TO THE GOVERNING AUTHORITIES"

The crucifixion of Jesus was the result of a legal-political judgment by Caesar's representative, whatever Pilate's personal motives may have been. Because faith understands this particular political verdict to be God's eschatological act of salvation, Jesus' death is the end of all hope of finding salvation through man's political activity.

Likewise, the resurrection of Jesus demonstrated to the last believer that the kingdom of God is brought about not by man's political action, or by his religious cooperation with God, but by God himself alone who raised Jesus from the dead. Jesus' followers may have attached their political expectations to him during his ministry, but such hopes came to naught at his cross. His resurrection could not revive them either because the resurrected one did not confront his unjust judges nor did he overthrow the oppressive "structures" of the Jewish theocracy or of the Roman Empire which brought him to the cross. The world after Easter went on as before.

Hence, to seek to develop a "political theology"[20] on the basis of the cross and the resurrection, as has recently been at-

20. Cf. J. Moltmann, *The Crucified God* (New York: Harper, 1974). In this book freedom of faith, which is God's work and gift, becomes suddenly political freedom from oppressive structures, which is and ought to be man's achievement. Moltmann could have remembered that, in spite

tempted, is an undertaking utterly foreign to the first century Christians. After Easter, they followed Jesus in suffering within the existing unjust "structures," but did not become enemies of the state in principle. In contrast to certain groups of modern theologians who, like the Zealots of old, are in love with religiously grounded revolutions, the early Christians knew that the freedom of faith is neither identical with nor dependent on political freedom and just social structures. Even when they experienced various forms of persecution, including martyrdom at the hands of Jews or pagans, they were conscious of the eschatological and nonpolitical foundation of their faith and witness.

The fact that their nonpolitical faith was considered to be a political threat by the existing powers did not demonstrate to Christians any political dimension of the gospel calling for revolution against those powers. It indicated rather the corruption and fear of the world in the presence of the powerlessness of Christ and of his followers. Their faith was grounded not in the weakness of political power, or in the compromise with which political power must always operate, but in the God who raises the dead. They believed that the powerlessness of the crucified Christ is the eschatological power of God unto salvation for Jews and gentiles alike.

Yet simultaneously, they did not become enemies of the state and its power politics. They regarded the state—be it Jewish or Roman—as the temporary ordinance of God within this world until that day when, through the actions of God and his Christ, suffering and death shall be no more. Only after we first radically distinguish God's eschatological action through Christ's cross and resurrection from man's political action of securing or changing the sociopolitical status quo, can we then proceed to discover how God's eschatological action, received as a gift, also interacts with and penetrates into man's quest for justice and liberty.

of persecutions, the early Christians did not become enemies of the oppressive empire in principle. Why not?—because for them the freedom of faith did not consist in programs of political liberation.

We shall turn to the letters of Paul in order to understand first the distinction and then the interaction between God's eschatological deed and human politics in the world.

The Law in Paul's Theology

Common to Saul the persecutor and Paul the apostle of Jesus Christ was the conviction that the message of the crucified and resurrected Jesus stands in contradiction to the law as way of salvation. Hence he persecuted the church before his conversion and he declared afterward that Christ is the "end of the law" (Rom. 10:4).

What did Paul mean by law? The apostle also affirmed what the former persecutor had believed, namely, that the law written in the Pentateuch is "holy, righteous, and good" (Rom. 7:12). However, in contradiction to his previous assumptions, the apostle held that the law cannot make man holy, righteous, and good in the sight of God. In comparison with other people, Paul could claim that he had been "blameless" as far as "righteousness under the law" was concerned (Phil. 3:6). In his case, the law had fulfilled the function of producing "righteousness under the law," that is, moral behavior among men and Paul did not deny the appropriateness of this function of the law as we shall see when we deal with Rom. 13:3–4.

Suffice it to point out that the apostle took it for granted that gentiles also who do not have the Moses Torah can do "by nature what the law [the Torah] requires" because the demands of the one law of God are written on their hearts. The moral deeds of gentiles demonstrated to Paul that even though they did not know the codified form of the law of God, they nevertheless know God's law in the form of the natural law. Its demands are in part fulfilled also by gentiles. But that is not all.

The insight that obedience to the Moses Torah cannot make man righteous before God dawned on Paul as a result of his encounter with the resurrected Christ. Then and only then could he understand the other function assigned to the law by God, namely, that the law "works wrath" (Rom. 4:15), that it multiplies transgressions (Gal. 3:19), that it places us under

God's judgment because it always finds us to be already sinners. Sinful man will always deceive himself (Rom. 7:11), and misuse the law for achieving his standing before God on the basis of his own performance of the law's demands (Rom. 9:31–10:4), as if he were not always already a sinner. The function of the Torah, therefore, is to "lock up" man in the prison of his sinfulness (Gal. 3:22–23) and to hold him thus accountable to God (Rom. 3:19).

Although the Torah was given to Israel only (Rom. 9:4), yet the gentiles also know God's demands (Rom. 2:14–15), even as "God's invisible nature which is his eternal power and deity" could be clearly perceived by them in and through his creation. Therefore the gentiles also "are without excuse" (Rom. 1:19–20). In spite of individual moral actions, they do not acknowledge and honor their Creator and they commit all kinds of abominable acts (Rom. 1:18–31). The law of God, known to Jew and gentile, condemns Jew and gentile alike (Rom. 3:19–20.

While Stoicism and Judaism seek freedom *through* the law, the apostle proclaims freedom *from* the law for those who are redeemed by Christ and who die with him to the law (Gal. 3:13; 2:19). The presupposition of freedom from the law is that Christ himself was under the law (Gal. 4:4). In receiving the judgment of the law (Gal. 3:13; 2 Cor. 5:21), he brought about "the end of the law."

This means that already now "there is no condemnation for those who are in Christ" (Rom. 8:1), and in the final judgment Christ himself, sitting at God's right hand, will intercede for all believers (Rom. 8:34) so that the condemnation of the law will come to nothing. Hence, anyone who rejects faith in God's salvation through Christ in favor of the law as means of salvation stands on the same level with pagans who serve the "elemental spirits of the universe" (Gal. 4:3, 9). Through the word of the cross, man's quest for self-realization gives way to faith.

Yet the believer who is free from legalism and from condemnation by the law, stands under "the law of Christ" (Gal.

6:2), under the demand of love which fulfills the law (Rom. 13:8–10). To "serve one another in love" (Gal. 5:13), because "God's love has been poured into our hearts through the Holy Spirit which has been given to us" (Rom. 5:5) constitutes for Paul the decisive demand laid upon those who are no longer slaves under the power of sin (Romans 6), but are incorporated through baptism into the body of Christ as "new creatures" (1 Cor. 12:13; 2 Cor. 5:17).

Note that the numerous Pauline ethical imperatives to love, serve, put on Christ, etc., are based upon the indicatives which speak of God's gracious act in a rich variety of ways. Fulfillment of these imperatives is not the condition of our acceptance by God, but the result of God's eschatological acceptance of us. For example, *because* God justifies the ungodly by grace through faith (Rom. 3:21–11:36), "*therefore,* present yourselves" to him and "do not be conformed" to the life-style and the thinking of this age (Rom. 12:1–2). Compare also Phil. 2:13 with 2:12; or Gal. 3:27 with Rom. 13:14; or Rom. 6:2 with 6:11; or 1 Cor. 5:6 with 5:7, etc. The new life received is to be expressed in and through the believers' lives.

The apostle saw in love not a virtue which can be achieved. Rather love is God's eschatological gift which must be expressed by those who are "in Christ," that is, by those whose lives are determined by Christ's cross, resurrection, and Spirit. Because love is an eschatological reality, as 1 Cor. 13:8–13 demonstrates, therefore it must constitute the bond among the members of God's eschatological avant garde, the church. Paul could show concretely what this means in particular situations, e.g., Rom. 12:3–14.

Two Realms and Two Times

However, those who have already been "delivered from this present evil age" (Gal. 1:4) are also still part of this world and its structures. While "the form of this world is passing away" (1 Cor. 7:31), it has not yet passed away. While believers are already in Christ, the consummation is yet to come (1 Corinthians 15). Hence, the Christian exists simultaneously in two times and in two realms.

He already exists in the eschatological time of God's love, righteousness, and peace which through the proclamation of the gospel breaks into the present age. But he does not yet live in the antithesis to this present age because his resurrection still lies in the future and suffering has not disappeared from his present.

To express it in spatial categories, Paul held that the believer has already been incorporated into the realm of Christ's body in which the differences of race, sex, and social status are abrogated. "There is neither Jew nor Greek, there is neither slave nor free, there is neither male nor female; for you are all one in Christ Jesus" (Gal. 3:28). Yet simultaneously, he lives in the structures of this world which are not yet part of Christ's body. Hence, he lives simultaneously in two times and in two realms.

The unity of the body of Christ is to be made manifest in love which expresses the solidarity of Christ's members which are different (1 Cor. 12:12–13:7). Love is also to be expressed toward the neighbor including the enemy (Rom. 12:14–21; 13:8–10). After all, "God showed his love for us . . . while we were enemies" (Rom. 5:8–10). For Paul the nature of love is defined christologically not in terms of the Torah, because love, in distinction to the Torah, is an eschatological reality. But the christologically defined demand of love also bestows new splendor on the commandments of the Decalogue (Rom. 13:8–16).

But how is the Christian to live in the structures of this world which is destined to pass away? Frequently, Paul is berated—or poorly defended—for his alleged social conservatism. On the basis of 1 Cor. 7:20, the vast majority of Pauline interpreters argue that according to Paul a Christian should *remain* "in the state," the position, the social station in which he finds himself. Stay as you are. Not even slaves, it is argued, should avail themselves of the opportunity to become free men, but rather they should remain slaves and stay as they are. This is the usual interpretation of 1 Cor. 7:20.

103

While the Greek text of 1 Cor. 7:21 permits such an interpretation, historically it would have been unthinkable that a slave who was manumitted could remain a slave. For this and other reasons, a young scholar recently proposed paraphrasing this verse: "But if, indeed, you become manumitted, by all means as a freedman live according to God's calling."[21] Moreover, he showed convincingly that the translations of the previous verse (1 Cor. 7:20) are also incorrect. The Greek word (*klēsis*) translated with "state" in the Revised Standard Version, meaning social station or position, must be translated with "God's call" which comes through the gospel. It does not refer at all to man's status in society.

What then is Paul talking about in 1 Cor. 7:17–22? God's eschatological call in Christ which comes through the gospel abolishes the distinction between Jew and Greek. Hence, Christians should not reintroduce them. Jewish Christians should not remove the marks of circumcision and gentile Christians should not be circumcised, not because such changes are prohibited, but because they are stupid and worthless in the sight of God. Their circumcised or uncircumcised status is unimportant in the church and before God. What is important is keeping God's commandments and remaining in the gospel, in God's call (7:17–20).

Likewise, Paul held that the social condition of being a slave does not imply an inferior standing before God nor does the social position of a freedman mean an advantage in the church or in the sight of him who called you. What is important is to remain in the gospel, in God's call, whether you are a slave or have the opportunity of being manumitted. How little Paul wished to forbid changing one's social status can be seen in that the unmarried can change their social status and get married, and that those married to unbelievers can divorce their spouses if they so desire (1 Cor. 7:15). Even though Paul him-

---

21. S. Scott Bartchy, *Mallon Chrēsai: First Century Slavery and the Interpretation of I Corinthians 7:21.* Society of Biblical Literature for the Seminar on Paul. Dissertation Series, no. 11 (Missoula, Mont.: University of Montana Printing Department, 1973), p. 183.

self preferred celibacy, he knew that not everyone has this particular charisma, even if everyone has his own charisma (1 Cor. 7:7).

However, God's calling does not imply the demand for asceticism and renunciation of sexual relations in marriage (7:2–6). Living like brother and sister, or like angels, is not what God's eschatological call in Christ is all about. God did not call people out of their bodily existence onto a road of spiritual withdrawal and asceticism, but he called us to faith while still in the body. Therefore, those who are married owe their spouses not only the eschatologically motivated agapē, but also sexual love (7:3) because they still live in this world and in the body. Paul, far from discouraging every kind of change in one's social status, was convinced that the word of the cross relativized every social status and simultaneously any social status should be the occasion of living in accordance with God's call, the gospel.

Precisely God's eschatological call which relativizes the social status enables Paul to speak of the believer's distance from the world and its social activities. "From now on, let those who have wives live as though they had none, and those who mourn as though they were not mourning, and those who rejoice as though they were not rejoicing, and those who buy as though they had no goods, and those who deal with the world as though they had no dealings with it" (1 Cor. 7:29–31).

These activities were not simply rejected by Paul. He himself could admonish: "Rejoice with those who rejoice, weep with those who weep" (Rom. 12:15). But these activities no longer determine the existence of believers, because their existence is and should be determind by God's call in Christ. The believer's involvement in the world must remain in tension with his freedom in Christ through whom he has already become part of the new creation. Hence, he can look with a certain detachment upon "this world which passes away" (1 Cor. 7:31), and he will avoid an idolatrous involvement as if the kingdom of God were identical with his activities in or against social structures.

This inner detachment which results from being in Christ

enables Paul to see and appreciate that which is good in the world. Because the believer is no longer determined by the world's ambitions, he is therefore free to acknowledge "what is good and acceptable and perfect" in the world (Rom. 12:2).

Paul therefore could appreciate ethical teachings which had their origin in an amazing variety of non-Christian traditions. Jewish popular wisdom is found side by side with Hellenistic rationalistic instruction. "Whatever is true, whatever is honorable, whatever is just, whatever is pure . . . lovely . . . gracious, if there is any excellence, if there is anything worthy of praise, think about these things" (Phil. 4:8). The apostle here as elsewhere (cf. Rom. 1:32; 2:14–15; 7:22) presupposes that what is good, true, and just can be known also by man apart from Christ, and he insists that it is to be realized in practice by the believer. To accept what is good, true, and just in the world does not imply "conformity to this age" (Rom. 12:2), but rather expresses the recognition of the universality of God's law which demands performance of God's will and which simultaneously condemns Adam as a sinner.

Therefore it is not surprising that the content of Paul's ethical demand is not new. What is new is the context. It is addressed to the man who has been "transformed by the renewal of your mind." The renewed reason is a reason dominated by the love of God which is in Christ Jesus, justifying the ungodly and liberating them from sin's enslaving power "that you may prove [approve, and perform] what is the will of God, what is good and acceptable and perfect" (Rom. 12:2).

The renewal of the reason does not imply that Christians are intellectually keener than others, but that they are able to recognize the destructive powers of the mind. They can and should point out the mind's perversion by nationalism, i.e., the "my-country-right-or-wrong" mentality and racism, by irrationalism and emotionalism, by self-centered quietism and individualistic isolationism, by benign neglect of the poor and demonization of the enemy, personal or national. While reason remains man's best tool for ordering this world, it is also man's great weapon for self-righteousness, oppression, and destruction.

Christians and the church know of sin's enslaving power, not because sin lies behind them, but because the struggle between "the flesh" and the spirit (Gal. 5:17), between the mind of Adam and the mind of Christ (Phil. 2:2–11) goes on and continues within the church and within the believer. They also know God's eschatological power of love in Christ which opens new horizons for our reason so that one can perceive fellow creatures and potential brothers in the enemies, a love which gives direction to reason, a love which liberates from self-righteousness, and spiritual isolationalism, a love which contributes to peace within the secular community "if possible, so far as it depends on you" (Rom. 12:18).

In short, the corporate reason of the church renewed by the Spirit proves and approves that which is true, just, and good in the world, and translates it into action as a deliberate response to belonging to Christ. The church which has already been delivered from this age, that is, from the condemnation of the law, from the power of sin, and from separation from God in death is required to express her faith and her renewed reason because the church is God's eschatological sign in and for this world.

Life in Social Structures

While the members of Christ's body are to practice love in interpersonal relations, they are admonished to show submission within the existing structures. In Paul's letters these structures are limited to marriage, the family and home, the institution of slavery, and the empire. Economics and politics lie outside the problems addressed in his letters.

In distinction to marriage or the state, Paul never regarded slavery as an ordinance of God. While Christian slaves of a pagan master knew that their social status is abrogated in Christ's body, Paul made it quite clear to the Christian slave-master, Philemon, that he expected him to treat his slave, Onesimus, as a brother "both in the *flesh* and in the Lord" (Philemon 16). In my opinion this means that Onesimus should be set free. Among the members of the body of Christ the unity in Christ has to be expressed also "in the flesh." The gospel of love interacts with an existing structure and robs it of its dreadfulness. Soon erstwhile slaves will become bishops of churches and from the end of the first century we hear of "many" Christians in Rome who delivered themselves into slavery in order to provide food for the needy or as ransom for fellow Christian slaves (1 Clement 55:2–3; Hermas simil. 1:8; mand. 8:10).

With respect to the empire Paul wrote that what is right for everybody is proper also for Christians: "Let every person be subject to the governing authorities." They are "instituted by God" and are his "ministers" and servants "for your good." Hence, pay your taxes and revenues, your respect and honor, and be "subject, not only to avoid God's wrath but also for the sake of conscience" (Rom. 13:1–7).

This text does not regard the state as an order of creation, but as an ordinance of God, the universal lawgiver. The purpose of the governmental authorities is to promote that which is good and punish that which is evil. The emphasis in this section does not lie on the state as such, but on Christians and their behavior within the state. The situation of conflict between demands made by Roman magistrates and the Christian conscience is not taken into consideration here because it had not arisen; Paul gave an ad hoc admonition and did not compose a treatise on the state. He could take it for granted that any Christian would know that obedience toward the authorities is always penultimate and, when conflicts arise, the Christian obeys God rather than men (Acts 5:29). Three points should be noted.

First, the "good" which the authorities are to promote is not the good of eternal salvation but of earthly preservation.[22] The "good" is therefore a relative entity. Paul himself had experienced the Roman system of Roman justice on his body. "Three times I have been beaten with the rods" ordered by Roman magistrates (2 Cor. 11:25), and he knew of Jesus' crucifixion

22. Contrary to J. T. Sanders (cited above, note 17), pp. 59–60 and p. 60, note 27. For other New Testament witnesses, see G. Krodel, "Church and State in the New Testament," *Dialog, a Journal of Theology* (Winter 1976).

by the Roman prefect, one of those governing authorities. When, in spite of the obvious injustices perpetrated by Caesar's "establishment," Paul could still call it "a servant of God for your good" and "a terror not to good conduct but to bad," then the relativity of these statements must be understood. The emperor Nero became a terror also to good conduct as pagans and Christians alike would testify a decade after Romans 13 was written.

These statements describe how God wants civil authorities to function. They ought to use their power for the promotion of justice and for the punishment of evildoers. Furthermore, Paul presents the basic claim of the empire and of every civil government in demythologized form, namely, that it uses its power for promoting justice and curbing evil. Finally, civil authority stands under the apocalyptic reservation (13:11–12). It is not a permanent but a temporary and hence transitory institution. Its structure may therefore not be absolutized. What is absolute is the demand for service to God also within the time-conditioned structures.

Second, the exhortation "to be subject" does not imply blind submission to the civil authorities and its demands. After all, when King Aretas issued a warrant for Paul's arrest, the apostle did not submit to this legitimate civil authority of Damascus but fled instead (2 Cor. 11:32–33). Submission must be in harmony with the Christian's conscience (v. 6) and therefore includes not just obedience, but also responsible action. Although the scope of responsible action in the structures of the empire was limited at that time, the apostle affirmed it because God seeks to curb evil and maintain justice through political power.

Third, the statement that the civil authorities are instituted by God may not be interpreted in terms of the legitimacy of their accession or in terms of the morality of the rulers. Nero, who was the governing authority when Romans 13 was written, came to power because his mother Agrippina, after talking emperor Claudius into adopting her son, poisoned Claudius. Claudius' own son Britannicus—by his third wife Messalina who was later executed as an adulteress—was poisoned shortly after

Nero's accession. Agrippina herself was murdered in 59 and Octavia, the daughter of Claudius whom Nero had married, was likewise murdered after Nero took Poppea as his mistress. Poppea, in turn, kicked by an enraged Nero, while she was expecting his child, hemorrhaged to death, only to be raised to divine honors afterward by a remorseful emperor. Nero's stepfather Claudius had become emperor because his predecessor Gaius, popularly known as Caligula, had been assassinated along with his wife by Praetorian officers, at which time their little daughter was smashed to pieces against a wall. Gaius himself had ascended the imperial throne through the intervention of the Praetorian guard. Legitimacy? Morality? Far from it!

When a disastrous fire ravaged ten of Rome's fourteen districts, Nero attempted to counteract persistent rumors that he himself had caused the fire, be it for his own amusement or for gaining space for his building programs. Intending to shift the blame to someone else, the emperor created a diversion and ordered the arrest and subsequent condemnation of Roman Christians. "Besides being put to death they [the Christians] were made to serve as objects of amusement; they were clad in the hides of beasts and torn to death by dogs; others were crucified, others were set on fire to illuminate the night." With others Nero staged "a show in the circus" (Tacitus, *Annales* 15, 44). Morality? Respect for law? Far from it!

At that time also Simon Peter probably lost his life. Paul who, as a Roman citizen, had appealed to Caesar (Acts 25:11–12) may actually have met Nero face to face a few years before the fire, or else he appeared before Nero's confidant Burrus who, as prefect of the Praetorian Guards, represented Nero in such matters. This encounter ended with Paul's execution and resulted in Nero's learning to distinguish between Jews and Christians, a distinction which his predecessor Claudius did not make when he expelled both from Rome in A.D. 49 (Suetonius, Claudius 25, 4; Acts 18:2).

Romans 13 does not constitute Paul's stamp of approval on Nero's tyrannical insanities and lusts, but speaks of the ordering power of civil authorities. Though always threatened by sin, the empire's power is delegated by God "for your good" and for the punishment of evil. That it perverts that power more often than not is no argument against its delegated function.

Because politics is always power politics and Christians must submit to it and not withdraw into isolation, therefore they indeed exist in two realms. They live in the realm of Nero whose God-given function is to punish evildoers and in the realm of Christ who justifies the ungodly. In a similar vein, the fourth evangelist distinguishes between the kingdom of God, the life, light, and truth which Jesus is and offers, and the earthly kingdom. "My kingship is not of this world," but the exercise of civil authority is "given you from above"—from God (John 18:36; 19:11).

The Empire as Beast

Romans 13 interpreted the emperor, governors, and magistrates of Rome as being the servants and ministers of God. Revelation 13 sees in them the manifestation of Satan, pictured as beast and as harlot. Already, prior to Revelation, apocalyptic Christians saw the planned erection of Caligula's statue in Jerusalem's temple and the subsequent destruction of the temple in A.D. 70 as manifestations of Satan in specific acts of blasphemy committed by the empire, acts which were believed to usher in the End (tradition behind Mark 13:14).

The apocalyptic interpretation of the empire finds its fullest form in the Revelation of St. John. Loyalty toward Rome, praying for the emperor (1 Tim. 2:1), submitting to (Rom. 13:1) or honoring the emperor (1 Pet. 2:17) have disappeared. The absolutized state which *demands* emperor worship is no longer God's ordinance but Satan's manifestation in history. Yet there are two important links with the rest of first century Christianity. One is the conviction of Christ's victory over the Satanic powers. Second there is no call to armed revolt in Christ's name. The judgment on the empire, also in the Book of Revelation, remains strictly God's action.

111

This apocalyptic tradition remained alive in the second century among Montanists and the Sibyline Oracles Book 8, but it was Romans 13 which became and remained normative in the Catholic Church. In spite of the perpetual legal insecurity, in spite of countless harassments, and in spite of occasional fierce persecutions, the church of the second century in general affirmed the empire as ordinance of God distinct from the body of Christ.

William H. Lazareth

Sentinels for
the Tricentennial

LUTHERANS COMMITTED TO JUSTICE

Christians cannot be worldly enough. Scripture admonishes us to live "in" but "not of" the world, and to help others do the same. In our day especially, worldly involvement has become the hallmark of authentic human existence. To be truly human is to be truly engaged in and for humanity.

It is therefore only through selfless encounter and passionate dialogue—with atheists, agnostics, secularists, Communists, or simply our current American supernationalists—that intellectual Christians may once again learn to out-think as well as out-bleed the world. For we are God's chosen instruments by whom others might find their maturity in Christ. This means that we are called not only to Christianize heathen, but also to humanize idolators. We proclaim that the Exemplar for true humanity, as well as true divinity, has been revealed in Jesus Christ, the Second Adam who inaugurated a new humanity based on a new testament with God.[1]

The Broken World

The brutal fact is that the twentieth century has been replete with ugly exhibits of man's inhumanity to his fellow men. Our breath-taking advances in scientific technology have been

1. See my fuller essay on "Sacred Secularity" included in *Humane Gesellschaft,* ed. Trutz Rendtorff and Arthur Rich (Furche: Zwingli, 1970).

matched only by our life-taking retreats in public morality. Astronauts float in palaces in outer space while citizens wallow in hovels in our inner cities. Never was there a time when a brilliant but broken world was more in need of the healing love of Christ's united disciples. Never was there a time when the stakes were higher and God's enemies stronger.

In our modern, sophisticated age, are we Christians still able to confess with the Seer John that there is a demonic whore at work, "the great whore of Babylon," who is still trying desperately to destroy the unity of the family of God? Surely the headlines of every daily newspaper shout out her seductive advances:

W for *War*—deadly military encounters from the swamps of Southeast Asia through the sands of the Middle East into the jungles of Africa, with thermonuclear superpowers poised to annihilate each other with the apocalyptic horrors of atomic overkill;

H for *Hunger*—three and a half billions of God's children in the world today, with an estimated one out of every three of them going to bed famished every night of their impoverished lives, and with over ten thousand persons dying daily of malnutrition and starvation;

O for *Overpopulation*—those three and a half billion souls expected to double to some seven billion within the next few decades before A.D. 2000, with eighty-five percent of these militant youth likely to come of age in the underdeveloped, revolution-ready countries of the third world—in Asia, Africa, and Latin America—most of whom already bitterly hate the "Christian West" as the religious legitimizers of their long-suffered colonialism and imperialism;

R for *Racism*—all the world looking anxiously toward the United States to see whether our democratic way of life is now facing a premature death in two separate and unequal societies, a death prompted by our sinful unwillingness to eradicate the white racism that violates the dignity and equality of all of God's children in this land of the not-so-free and home of the not-so-brave;

E for *Eco-crisis*—our plundered planet being compulsively ravaged as six percent of the world's people in the North Atlantic community gorge ourselves on about fifty percent of the world's available resources.

It is this multifaceted "whore of Babylon"—war, hunger, overpopulation, racism, and eco-crisis—which poses the chief threats to the bride of Christ, the church, as she tries to love a broken world as she herself has been loved by her divine Beloved. Hence, those of us who confess the lordship of Christ cannot dismiss the anguish of God's children with merely a sociological shrug of the shoulders.

The New Testament reveals a demonic dimension in our inhumanity to our fellow men. St. Paul warns: "We are not contending against flesh and blood, but against the principalities, against the powers, against the world rulers of this present darkness, against the spiritual hosts of wickedness in the heavenly places" (Eph. 6:12). By way of contrast, Scripture also witnesses to a godly dimension in our responsible care of our neighbors. As Jesus promised, "Truly, I say to you, as you did it to one of the least of these my brethren, you did it to me" (Matt. 25:40). In other words, the church's social ministry is an integral part of the ongoing mission of God's Son as he struggles against the dethroned, but not yet destroyed, forces of evil in this fallen world.

The Worldly Mission of Christ's Church

Our position rests on the conviction that Christian faith in the Triune God expresses itself in a distinctively evangelical social ministry. It is rooted in the proclamation of God the Redeemer (*kerygma*), nourished in the fellowship of God the Sanctifier (*koinonia*), and bears fruit in the world of God the Creator (*diakonia*). Our Trinitarian faith determines the quality and direction of Christian service, whether believers are gathered about God's Word or scattered throughout God's world.

This Trinitarian stance also demands that we boldly challenge a good deal of the acculturated religiosity that now parades under the glamorous title of "worldly Christianity." The ambiguity in the currently popular slogan of "worldly Christianity" is rooted in the New Testament. If we grant some linguistic latitude in scriptual usage, there are two different Greek words that generally can be translated into English as "world": *kosmos* and *aion*. In the realm of creation, the "world" can refer to God's created universe (*kosmos*). In the realm of redemption, the "world" can also express the opposition between old age (*aion*) of disobedient creatures in Adam and the new age (*aion*) of faithful disciples in Christ. So, to illustrate, "For God so loved the world (*kosmos*) that he gave his only Son," as in the Gospel of John. However, "Do not be conformed to this world (*aion*), but be transformed by the renewal of your mind," as in Paul's Romans.

The risen Christ is destined to rule over all creation, over God's enemies, as well as over death (1 Cor. 15:20–28). At present, however, his redemptive rule extends only as far as there are persons who submit to him by God's grace through faith (Rom. 3:21–27). Simultaneously, his conflict still continues against those demonic principalities and powers that have been already dethroned, but not yet destroyed, in God's victory in his cross (Col. 2:8–15).

Applied concretely to political and military ethics, Paul's eschatological reservation ("not yet") and pastoral reservation ("by faith apart from works") combine to forbid any fanatical identification of the inbreaking new age in Christ with our morally ambiguous political and military activities for social justice. So, for example, the Pauline answer to current liberation theology is not quietistic theology but liberation ethics. This is affirmed in fidelity to the Christ who meant what he said to the Pilates and the anti-Pilates of all ages: "My kingship is not of this world" (John 18:36).

In view of this crucial distinction at the heart of New Testament faith, God's people now stand at a crucial crossroad. In response to the challenge for a more "worldly" and "relevant" Christianity, many American churches are dramatically abandoning their traditional divorce between the realms of the sacred and the secular.

Our thesis is that such congregations are thereby confronted with a great danger as well as an even greater opportunity:

(1) The danger is a new *kosmos*-oriented Christian humanism. This view is based on a man-centered "theology of glory." It seeks to show how Christians can "secularize their religion" in uncritical celebration of the "secular city" of man. Here there is an uneschatological identification of the realms of creation and redemption.

(2) In opposition, there is the opportunity to embrace a more humane Christianity that is aware of the *two aions* represented by the disobedient Adam and the Christ obedient unto death. This view should reflect a Christ-centered "theology of the cross." It should try to demonstrate how Christians can help to "sacralize the profane" in faithful testimony to the "eternal city" of God. Here there remains the eschatological distinction—without separation—of the realms of creation and redemption.

For those worldly theologians who are oriented solely to one immanent *kosmos,* certainly God—if he be transcendent and Triune—must be dead. But for those worldly theologians who interpret God's *kosmos* in terms of *two aions,* the living God's creative and redemptive activity among humanity is more necessary than ever.

Our plea is for Lutheran Christians to maintain their ecclesial integrity amid more intensive social ethical involvements. We are the servant church of a Servant Lord who is always identified with—but never identical to—the poor, the suffering, the oppressed, "the least of these my brethren" in our unjust societies. The church's greatest challenge today is to preserve its identity in the gospel of Christ even as it identifies with the needy of the world.

There is a growing alliance of strange theological bed-fellows in support of various kinds of "Christianized" humanism that smack of syncretistic universalism. One common denominator is often the cosmic significance of the Christ-event (usually the Incarnation) which supposedly has ontological effects of reconciliation and unity on all men whether they know it or not, or confess it in faith or not (Barth).

Secular triumphalism easily replaces ecclesial triumphalism under the various slogans of "cosmic Christology" (Chardin), "christological universalism" (Tillich), "anonymous Christianity" (Rahner), "transfiguration of history" (Berdyaev), "secular city" (Cox), and "liberation theology" (Gutiérrez). Nevertheless, the apostolic claim—that the good news of God springs from a particular people, a particular set of events, a particular collection of documents, but that it is of universal significance, addressed to a universal audience, and seeks a universal allegiance—has always been and continues to be a scandal, a stumbling block, an offense (1 Cor. 1:23).

Is it not a special calling of Lutherans to make the unpopular biblical witness that Christ-centered reconciliation and unity must always be viewed dialectically in the light of God's mercy and judgment? While all men are sinners before a righteous God, not all men are victims in an unjust society. This demands that we clearly distinguish, without falsely separating or identifying, the church and the world.

Our Christian hope lies neither in the secularization of church nor the sacralization of the world. Rather the church's worldly posture must remain in eschatological tension. It is nonpartisan in faith as it serves all sinners alike in its ministry of Word and sacraments; yet it is also passionately partisan in love as it struggles on behalf of the victims of society in its ministry of freedom and justice.

Civil Righteousness

As an evangelical prophet, Luther gave primary emphasis to the religious dimension of human existence under the rule of God's gospel. This realm Luther describes variously as "the kingdom of God," "the kingdom on God's right hand," "the kingdom of Christ and the gospel," and "man before God."

What is of special interest for us here, however, is the way in which all of this is related by Luther to the second of the two kingdoms: "the kingdom of Caesar and the law," "the kingdom on God's left hand," and "man in community life." Luther asserts with Paul that the ethical dimensions of human existence is properly under the reign of God's law whose religious function of condemning sin is always coupled with its political function of promoting justice.

This strategy for the political involvement of Christians is supported by the underdeveloped, and relatively unfamiliar, views of Martin Luther with regard to civil righteousness and natural law.[2]

> To put it as briefly as possible here, Paul says that the law is given for the sake of the unrighteous, that is, that those who are not Christians may through the law be externally restrained from evil deeds. Since, however, no one is by nature Christian or pious, but every one sinful and evil, God places the restraints of the law upon them all, so that they may not dare give rein to their desires and commit outward, wicked deeds. (Weimar edition [*WA*] 11, 250)

The indispensable key to Luther's understanding of the "kingdom of the world" is his conviction that God has ordained civil authority ". . . to restrain the un-Christian and wicked so that they must keep the peace outwardly, even against their will" (*WA* 11, 251). This means that God in his loving providence has so structured daily life in the civil community that all persons—"even against their will"—are constrained to live in conformity with at least a minimal standard of social morality if only out of the fear of punishment or hope of reward.

In comparison with Christian righteousness, of course, this so-called civil righteousness (*iustitia civilis*) comes off a very poor second. Whereas Christian righteousness springs forth from faith, and is therefore joyful and willing, civil righteousness is forced out of unbelief, and is consequently "murmuring" and involuntary. Since "all that does not proceed from faith is sin" (Romans 14, 23), civil righteousness has absolutely no justify-

2. Cf. the expanded chapter on "Righteousness and Social Justice" in my *Luther on the Christian Home* (Philadelphia: Fortress, 1960), pp. 115 ff.

ing value—no matter how enlightened its self-interest might be. It is "inherently vicious" at the core, however attractive its surface (*WA* 40, 2; 526).

Luther remains unequivocal in his religious condemnation of all social ethical behavior which is not fired by the loving heart of one who has confessed Christ as his Lord and Savior. "Where there is only secular rule or law, there, of necessity, is sheer hypocrisy, though the commandments be God's very own. Without the Holy Spirit in the heart, no one becomes really pious, he may do as fine works as he will" (*WA* 11, 252).

Yet parallel with the many statements which condemn all civil righteousness as sinful in the sight of God, other writings of Luther consider the moral efforts of unregenerate persons to be relatively "righteous" in the realm of creation, even when they remain wholly unacceptable in the realm of redemption.

For instance: Although hating and killing might be considered equally sinful in heaven, it is clearly the lesser of two evils if society can at least compel a person to control murderous actions even if not hateful thoughts. In a fallen and sinful world, ethics must often be satisfied with the imperfect second-best. Consequently, God punishes sin with sin and employs sinful individuals and institutions as imperfect dikes against even more demonic expressions of a person's unfaithful rebellion against the Lord. "God is himself the founder, lord, master, demander, and rewarder of both spiritual and civil righteousness. There is no human order or power which is not a godly thing" (*WA* 19, 629–630).

Works of civil righteousness, therefore, fall on the boundary line between the two kingdoms as ultimately evil, but provisionally good; they are products of sin which are at once remedies against it. "Learn here to speak of the law as contemptuously as you can in matters of justification [*in causa iustificationis*] . . . but apart from justification [*extra locum iustificationis*], we ought with Paul to think reverently of the law, to commend it highly, to call it holy, righteous, good, spiritual, and divine" (*WA* 40, 1; 558).

Perhaps the most cogent illustration of Luther's ambivalent

attitude toward civil righteousness is the unexpected way in which he lauds the social expressions of goodness which natural reason and common sense can effect—apart from the gospel—for a just and peaceful society. Luther was convinced that all God's rational creatures—despite sin—are still capable of a high degree of civil righteousness by virtue of the divine law which God has written "with his own finger" into their hearts at creation (*WA* 10, 3; 373).

Even the most cursory reading of Luther's writings reveals a surprising number of references to the distinction between God's twofold rule by law and gospel in the two kingdoms, and the admirably high position afforded human reason when it is employed in the service of neighbors and limited to managing the technical affairs of everyday life (*WA* 10, 3, 380; *WA* 16, 251, 353).

> Here you must separate God from man, eternal matters from temporal matters. Involving other people, man is rational enough to act properly and needs no other light than reason. Consequently, God does not bother to teach men how they are to build houses, or make clothes, or marry, or make war, or sail a boat. For all such matters, man's natural light is sufficient. But in divine matters, such as man's relation to God and how God's will is fulfilled for our eternal salvation, here man's nature is completely stone-blind. (*WA* 10, 1, 1, 531)

In marked consistency with his earlier teachings is Luther's systematic portrayal of the proper exercise of reason and force to achieve social order and civil justice in his *Sermons on Exodus* (1524–1527). In the first place, there must be a clear distinction between the realms of creation and redemption, the kingdom of men and the kingdom of God.

> You have often heard of the differences between religious and civil authority. In the spiritual realm men are ruled by God through Christ as the head of all believers, although neither Christ nor the believers are ever openly seen. In the civil realm Christ does not exercise his rule directly, for he has delegated his powers to human rulers who are to govern their citizens in moderation, justice, and equity. (*WA* 16, 352)

In the second place, the nonredemptive rule of the sword in

the kingdom of men is aimed at the establishment of a just and orderly society in which men may live in peace and the gospel might be proclaimed unto the ends of the earth.

> Here we have described for us how the people of Israel were united together under a civil government and how that government was organized. [Moses] attends first to the civil authority before ordering the religious authority. . . . This is because the civil sword must first be exercised to secure peace and order on earth before anyone can preach with the necessary time, place, and tranquility. When men are compelled to take up spears, guns, and swords in time of strife, there is little opportunity to preach God's Word. (*WA* 16, 353)

In the third place, the nonredemptive rule and maintenance of the civil realm should be governed by a judicious use of reason and common sense which is implanted by God into every human being. In public office, personal piety is no substitute for political prudence. As Luther was to insist so often later, "Better a wise Turk than a foolish Christian," when it comes to running the state for the social welfare of all.

> God has placed man's civil life under the dominion of natural reason which has ability enough to rule physical things. Reason and experience together teach man how to do everything else that belongs to sustaining a life here on earth. These powers have been graciously bestowed by God upon man's reason, and we need not look to Scripture for advice in such temporal matters. God has seen to it that even the heathen is blessed with the gift of reason to help him live his daily life. (*WA* 16, 353)

Finally, Christians should be vigilant and not mix the two kingdoms by demanding of pagans in the kingdom of the world what is possible only among Christians in the kingdom of God. Luther insisted that "the world cannot be run by the gospel. . . . The sheep, to be sure, would keep the peace and would allow themselves to be fed and governed in peace, but they would not live very long" (*WA* 11, 252). Rather than attempt any naive and fruitless "Christianization" of the fallen social structures in the community, Christ's followers should dedicate their consecrated brains to learn even from pagans how best to live their daily lives so as to achieve the most equitable society possible under human reason, justice, law, and order.

> Pagans have been found to be much wiser than Christians. They have been able to order the things of this world in a far more capable and lasting way than have the saints of God. As Christ said, "The children of this world are wiser in their own generation than the children of light." They know how to rule external affairs better than St. Paul or other saints. It is because of this that the ancient Romans had such glorious laws and ordinances . . . without any counsel or guidance from Holy Scripture or the apostles. (*WA* 16, 354)

Consequently, without at all weakening the distinction between the two kingdoms, Luther can gratefully view all the provisional victories of dedicated men over hunger, sickness, crime, and social evils in general, as "signs" and foretastes of the coming kingdom of God when the rule of Christ will be all in all. Political peace and social justice remain qualitatively inferior to the peace of God and his righteousness, but—like the long finger of John the Baptist in Grünewald's "Crucifixion"—they point to the coming kingdom even while not yet a part of it.

Critics of Luther's alleged "cultural quietism" would do well to read Luther himself to challenge their unexamined prejudices.

> Just as the spiritual government or office should instruct people how to act in relation to God concerning their eternal salvation, so too the civil government should rule people so as to insure that man's body, goods, wife, children, household, and all his possessions remain in peace and safety for his earthly happiness. For God would have civil government become a prefiguration [*Vorbild*] of the true blessedness of his heavenly kingdom. (*WA* 51, 241)

The Law of Nature

Just as Luther was able to subsume all the Christian righteousness of the kingdom of God under the loose heading of "the law of Christ," so he often included everything that we have described heretofore as civil righteousness within the kingdom of men under the general rubric of "the law of nature" (*lex naturae*). This ambiguous designation has caused untold grief in Luther research ever since, for it is at once obvious from the theological foundations of his ethics that Luther could not possibly have meant by this term what it had traditionally stood for in the Aristotelian categories of Roman Catholic moral philosophy.

Perhaps most helpful today is Gustaf Aulén's suggestion that we first incorporate the material to which this tradition-laden term refers into Luther's overarching doctrine of the Two Kingdoms of creation and redemption. If we then interpret it in terms of "the law of creation," we readily divest it of any non-Christian metaphysical coloration and relate it directly to the ongoing creative activity of God in his temporal rule of the kingdom of the world. This certainly preserves the religious intention behind Luther's usage of a term whose meaning has become radically secularized for us since the godless philosophical inroads of the eighteenth century.[3]

In general, we may safely say that Luther conceived of the relation between "natural law" and "the law of Christ" in dialectical terms of radical correction and fulfillment. They reflect precisely the same provisional opposition and ultimate unity as between law and gospel, justice and love, reason and revelation, creation and redemption. In short, they are but another expression of the twofold way in which the Triune God governs his children as both their Creator and Redeemer.

Luther's doctrine of the bondage of human will and reason to the forces of evil, precluded any possibility of anyone living a righteous life apart from Christ. Yet, even sinners remain creatures of God who bear within their hearts in however distorted and corrupted a form a knowledge of the law of their

---

3. Cf. Gustaf Aulén, *The Faith of the Christian Church* (Philadelphia: Fortress, 1948), p. 189:

The idea *lex naturae* has often appeared as a substitute for the *lex creationis,* or *lex creatoris,* of Christian faith. *Lex naturae*, the law of nature, could be described as a rationalized and secularized variety of *lex creationis*. The foundation of both is a universal law. The difference between them can be defined in this way, that *lex naturae* is a metaphysical conception, while *lex creationis* is a religious concept, originating in the relation to God and inseparably connected with faith in God as Creator.

Creator. Persons in rebellion no longer possess a saving knowledge of God, but they still have consciences which witness to the contradiction between right and wrong. They still are rationally cognizant of the "law of nature" which tells them that "we should do good and avoid evil," that good is rewarded and evil punished, and that we must do good to others if we want to be treated well in return (*WA* 10, 1, 1, 203). For Luther, the ethic of natural law is the morality of the "Golden Rule."

> It is unrighteous in God's sight for me to refuse to serve my neighbor in need for I am then unjustly depriving him of what the Lord has provided for his benefit. I am obligated to treat him according to the natural law, "Do unto others as you would have them do unto you" [Matt. 7, 12]. And as Christ said, "Give to him who begs from you" [Matt. 5, 42]. (*WA* 10, 3, 291)

These words introduce us concretely to the ambiguity in Luther's view of civil righteousness or natural law morality. In some instances he clearly subordinates natural law to Christian love, while in others he couples the two so closely together as almost to equate them. For Luther, it would seem that social justice is the necessary form which Christian love takes in a given situation while yet falling short of the disinterested, sacrificial love (*agapē*) which God revealed in Christ.

The following quotation illustrates the one side of his position; namely, that justice is a sub-Christian, pagan virtue. Here it is emphasized that to love each other as we would like to be loved in return (Matthew 7, 12) is qualitatively inferior to loving each other as Christ has loved us (John 13, 34–35).

> The lepers here teach us faith while Christ teaches us love. Love does for the neighbor as it has seen Christ do for us. As he said, "For I have given you an example, that you also should do to others as I have done to you. . . . By this all men will know that you are my disciples, if you have love for one another" [John 13, 15, 35]. . . . Love does not fight or dispute; it is there only to do good. For this reason love always does more than it is obligated to do, going beyond the demands of the law. Consequently, St. Paul says that among Christians there should be no need for recourse in the civil law courts since love does not seek or stress its own rights, but desires only to do good to others [I Cor. 6, 1]. (*WA* 8, 360, 364)

125

On the other side, there are many important passages in Luther which lend great weight to the view that civil justice is the social expression of Christian love. Just as the "Golden Rule" is itself incorporated into the Sermon on the Mount, so too the Christian life in the temporal kingdom should be governed by the natural law of equity and moderation. Here followers of Christ join their nonbelieving neighbors in doing good to all men although their motivation is radically different. One of Luther's 1522 sermons on Philippians 4, 4–7 gives us a striking example of this "Christianized" natural law ("equity") which should govern Christians in their temporal pursuits.

> The word the Apostle uses here [*epieikeia, equitas, clementia, commoditas*] is perhaps best rendered as "leniency." This is a virtue by which man is guided to treat others with fairness and equity, and through whose practice man avoids setting himself up as the final rule and judge. Leniency permits men to distinguish between strict and merciful law, and to moderate that which is too strict: this is *equitas*. (*WA* 10, 1, 2, 174)

Luther is referring here to the classical medieval distinction between positive law (*iustum*) and natural law (*aequum*). Here the spirit of the law softens and qualifies the rigid application of the letter of the law, whenever its strict enforcement would do more harm than good in a concrete case. Natural law is the source and norm under which all human laws are to be held accountable. It is ". . . the heart and the empress of all laws, the fountain from which all law flows forth" (*WA, Tr.* 6, 6955). And yet at other times, meaning apparently the very same thing, Luther can call love ". . . the judge of all laws and their sound understanding" (*WA* 8, 664). Love is the "queen and mistress" which should ". . . govern all external civil laws in the world" (*WA* 17, 2, 92).

When pressed for a more specific description, however, Luther will go no further than seeing deeply embedded within natural law an abiding concern for the welfare of the neighbor.[4]

---

4. As a faithful biblical theologian, Luther has Paul to thank for his dilemma. It is the same Paul who condemns all non-Christian behavior in Romans 1 who is here testifying to God's universal law by lauding the pre-Christian moral virtues of the Greeks in Philippians 4.

"There should be a moderation in life which mitigates, adapts, and guides our capacities and behavior so that we feel constrained to be good, follow, shun, do, leave, and suffer in keeping with our neighbor's needs, even if it is at the cost of goods, honor, or personal comfort" (*WA* 10, 1, 2, 174–175).

After citing several examples of such "equity" in the lives of Christ, Peter, and Paul, Luther concludes: ". . . nothing else is necessary for a Christian but faith and love, with love determining what is to be done or not done according to its contribution to society" (*WA* 10, 1, 2, 176).

Since Luther himself complained that "we invent many fables about law" (*WA* 56, 355), we shall perhaps have to conclude that at different times and places Luther was treating various dimensions of this central ethical paradox: As two parallel lines meet only at infinity, the forces of love and law meet only in eternity.

In terms of our presentation, the morality of natural law may be viewed as part of the "strange work" (*opus alienum*) of God's nonredemptive activity under the law. Underneath the distorted mask of Aristotle's "law of nature," there is concealed the loving Creator of all mankind whose will is that all men should love one another. "The law of nature lives in us as heat and fire in flint. Its use is like that of a mirror, for it cannot be separated from the law of God" (*WA, Tr.* 2, 2243).

Prophetic Christians

We have briefly sketched Luther's views of civil righteousness and natural law. Now we might well conclude by suggesting the contemporary relevance of the Reformer's position after it has been properly "demedievalized."[5]

Karl Barth has properly exposed the "soft underbelly" of Lutheran social ethics in the realm of creation. Lutherans have been far more responsible in the realm of redemption. They have rightly stressed the redemptive significance of Christ, grace,

---

5. Cf. my "Luther's 'Two Kingdoms' Ethic Reconsidered" in *Christian Social Ethics in a Changing World*, ed. John C. Bennett (New York: Association, 1966), pp. 121, 130–131.

Scripture, faith, and the gospel. But in evangelical zeal they have often neglected the crucial importance of the nonredemptive counterparts: Caesar, nature, tradition, reason, and the law. Lutherans must quickly recapture and boldly champion the Reformer's appreciation of the "sacred secularity" of civil life, which is at once free from church-rule and yet subject to God-rule.

In attempting to translate Luther's theology into the twentieth century, we must never forget to shift the ethical accent, since his chief enemy was clericalism, whereas ours in secularism. *Luther had to put the church back under God's gospel; we must put the state and society back under God's law.*

Let no one underestimate the difficulty of this mission. Yet many unnecessary obstacles might be removed at the outset if Christians would properly distinguish the gospel of redemption from the law of creation, and then further differentiate the law's theological function to condemn sin from its political function to promote justice. Especially in our pluralistic culture, men and women who cannot worship together under the gospel must find more ways in which they can work together under the law. In mapping out the terrain, Christian social ethics can perform an incomparable service.

For example, is there not a "hard core" of nonredemptive morality in what Lutherans call "civil righteousness," what Calvinists call "common grace," what recent ecumenical statements call "middle axioms," what Roman Catholics call "natural law," what Jews call "social justice" and what secularists call "enlightened self-interest"? Even Karl Barth was compelled to admit, "It cannot be denied, however, that in the lists of examples [of ethical guidelines] quoted, we have more than once made assertions which have been justified elsewhere on the basis of natural law."[6] Well, as Shakespeare said, ". . . a rose, by any other name, would smell as sweet."

Lutherans are now challenged to make their contribution to this mighty ecumenical effort. Our traditional concentration on

6. Karl Barth, *Community, State and Church: Three Essays* (New York: Doubleday Anchor, 1960), p. 180.

the gospel has energized a sound personal ethic: "faith active in love." But the vast realm of corporate structures and institutional life has often thereby been deprived of the normative judgment and guidance of God's law by the church's neglect of a corresponding social ethic: "love working for justice." Though responsible for the proclamation of the whole Word of God, Lutherans have generally put much stronger emphasis on the personal appropriation of God's gospel (for politicians and economists) than on the social demands of God's law (for politics and economic life).

In short, what Lutherans need desperately today is a *prophetic* counterpart of the priesthood of all believers. Evangelical Christians will be reverent to God's Word as well as relevant to God's world by expressing both their priestly "Yes," through faith active in love, and their prophetic "No," through love working for justice.

Wordly Discipleship

One thing is certain: the people of God's new testament will rightly be rejected by the world, if we are not willing to face up to the revolutionary forces in faith and life whirling about us. Virtually everything is up for grabs today: "demythologizing" in theology, the pill, LSD and DNA in medicine, "black power" and "white backlash" in race relations, "escalation" and ICBM's in nuclear warfare, automation and cybernetics throughout industrial life, to say nothing of moon landings and potential underwater cities in our explorations of the frontiers of the universe.

As the twentieth century experiences the painful birth pangs of an awesome new age in human civilization, the church must quickly and gladly identify itself—even without all the pat answers—out in that broken world "where the action is." The essence of that unfaithfulness from which we all suffer in varying degrees is the beguiling ethos of religious withdrawal, cultural noninvolvement, and political isolationism. If the apostles have anything special to say to their American Lutheran heirs today, it might well be this: "The world is right; you're not worldly enough!"

For what else is the Incarnation of Christ but a personal parable of the holy worldliness of the love of God? What else is the gospel but the good news that, in Christ, God has identified himself with the totality of man's worldly existence? What else is the church but the contemporary embodiment of God's worldly commitment and worldly involvement?

The world is not here for the sake of the church; the church —as its Lord—is here for the sake of the world. Therefore life cannot be divorced into realms of "sacred" and "secular." God's new testament community will lose credibility to the extent to which it belies its "sacred secularity" by withdrawing into a shell of cultic security, and avoiding its conflict with the enemies of God on their territory, in their language.

When it comes to proclaiming the gospel we must always be both reverent to God's Word—compromising nothing, and yet relevant to God's world—adapting everything. Our Lord was no champion of the ghetto. The Good Shepherd is willing to leave the ninety-nine safe sheep and go out to regain the one that is lost. How much more necessary this is in our day when we, proportionately, have the ninety-nine lost sheep in the wilderness and still fondle the one little lamb who is already safely in the fold!

We recall the lethargy-shaking words of Jesus' prayer to the Father:

> "I have given them thy word; and the world has hated them because they are not of the world . . . I do not pray that thou shouldst take them out of the world, but that thou shouldst keep them from the evil one. . . . As thou didst send me into the world, so I have sent them into thy world." (John 17)

The answer to the world's false secularism is a restoration of the church's sacred secularity, a recovery of that holy worldliness of God's baptized people in ministering to sinful and forlorn men where they actually are: If God so loved the *world* that he sent his only Son to serve in it and die for it, how dare his disciples attempt to isolate themselves apart from life in the vain attempt for some kind of counterfeit self-sanctification?

The risen Christ with whom we live in the church is also the crucified Christ with whom we must die in the world. It is deep in the midst of life that God's suffering servant calls us to take up our cross and follow him. Secular man couldn't care less about "finding a gracious God" (Luther), but he is searching desperately for some gracious neighbors. Therefore our real question today is not, What should Christians be doing *in the church*? It is rather, What should they be doing *as the church* . . . in the broken world of God?

LUTHERANS ORGANIZED FOR JUSTICE

The distinctive approach of Lutherans to the Christian church is marked by both reverence and freedom: reverence because Chirst is there, freedom because much that is not Christ is also there. Lutherans revere the church because they cannot separate it from Christ. Yet they also feel free to reform the church because they do not identify it with Christ. Just as Christians are "at once righteous and sinful," so the Christian church is likewise "at once holy and sinful."

It should therefore be said at the outset that no Lutheran worth his salt could ever have more than a "lover's quarrel" with the church. Current talk of "Jesus people" organizing a "no-church movement" borders on blasphemy. This is because Lutherans believe that the church and its means of grace are the creation and gifts of God's Holy Spirit. Only in the church do persons find forgiveness of sin, life, and salvation. It would therefore be impossible for Lutherans to separate faithful discipleship from responsible churchmanship.

Still, the Lutheran's priestly "Yes" to the church is always balanced by a prophetic "No." It is the special calling of those trained in Christian theology to hold the church's faith and life accountable to God's sovereign Word, the proclamation of the law and the gospel. The Christian church, sinful as well as holy, is in need of continual self-examination and reformation. It remains the church of Christ because, and only insofar as, it remains faithful to the gospel of God's self-revelation.

Lutherans now face a peculiar challenge as they try to "speak the truth in love" in advocating social justice with Christians of other churches. To pose the dilemma as boldly as possible: As members of a church which believes that it certainly—though not exclusively—confesses the one true faith in Jesus Christ, can Lutherans avoid the twin pitfalls of sectarianism and "civil religion"? Can divided churchmen in a pluralistic culture be at once evangelical, ecumenical and ethical in their faithful witness to God's "left-hand" lordship in society?

Lutheran Christianity

What are the distinctive marks of Lutheran Christianity?[7] Generalizations are always hazardous because of the exceptions they overlook. Sweeping assertions are usually unfair to someone. Nevertheless, Holy Scripture admonishes us to try to read the "handwriting on the wall" and perceive the "signs of the times." In terms of both evangelical depth and catholic breadth, Lutherans at best have been *pastoral, confessional,* and *liturgical.*

In the first place, the Lutheran Church has had a *pastoral* concern for the individual soul. It has always been ready to proclaim God's law and gospel in order to grant disobedient and troubled persons Christ's pardon for their sin and the Spirit's power for their renewal. A strong ministry of serving love has also resulted in hundreds of homes, agencies, and institutions in which Christian compassion is shown to the weak, the old, the sick, and the oppressed. It is probably no accident that Lutherans prefer to call their clergy "pastor," and that there is no real equivalent in English for *Seelsorge.* This pastoral "care of souls" is a characteristic feature of the conscientious Lutheran minister. The pastor has a personal concern for each individual sheep whom he or she has been called by God to shepherd into eternal life.

Second, Lutheran theology has been soundly *confessional* in proclaiming Jesus Christ as Lord. As members of the mother

---

7. Cf. the author's extended chapter entitled "The Future of American Lutheranism" in *Protestant Churches and Reform Today,* ed. William J. Wolf (New York: Seabury Press, 1964).

church of the Reformation, Lutherans have always been called on to justify the "tragic necessity" of that great restoration of evangelical faith and life to the rest of the corrupted body of Christ. More recently, Lutherans have also had to disassociate themselves from those periodic outbursts of civic religiosity which likewise bear so little resemblance to the scriptural Word of God. The multitude of so-called Protestant sects and cults in the United States demonstrates clearly that human religion remains the chief enemy of God's revelation. Confessional theology, firmly centered in the good news of the New Testament, has been a hallmark of the Lutheran evangelical tradition.

Finally, the Lutheran Church has been *liturgical* in its sensitivity to good order and reverence in its adoration of the living God. The church's conservative reformation was concerned with eliminating only those objectionable features of the Roman Mass which belied the Christ-centered character of authentic Christian worship. All other churchly ceremonies, symbols, and appointments which serve faith as channels of the gospel were gladly kept and treasured as worthy means to praise God's holy name. Whether simple or elaborate, the church's liturgy has been gratefully respected by the worshiping community.

Pastoral, confessional, liturgical: these key features are most typical of the faith and life of Lutheran Christianity. That is the ideal Lutherans strive after, the way they hope to witness to God at their best. But life is lived in the actual, and not the ideal. These goals are far easier to preach than to practice. In the light of these three distinguishing characteristics, let us now hazard an overall look at American Lutheranism. Where has it been, and how has this affected its political responsibility in society?

Lutherans in America

At the expense of distorted oversimplification, I would suggest that American Lutherans in the past have often overemphasized their Lutheran accent at the expense of their evangelical catholicity.

This ecclesiastical provincialism is understandable, even if not wholly justifiable. Lutheran churches were largely immigrant churches, and they usually tried to maintain their familiar languages, customs, and way of life in their new home-away-from-home. Many of them were dissenters from the dominant religious traditions of the established churches of their native soil. They felt threatened in a new country when challenged by all kinds of strange peoples, beliefs, and practices. It was only natural that many of these German and Scandinavian Pietists gradually withdrew into the security of small, ethnically homogeneous communities. As a temporary, transitional maneuver, this defensive stance had much to commend it. Its indefinite perpetuation, however, exacted a heavy toll on American Lutheranism's "characteristic" (but un-Lutheran!) way of life.

First, pastoral care for the person often degenerated into a kind of ecclesiastical *individualism*. There was very little concern for the church outside the walls of the local congregation. Charity not only began, but often ended, right at home. Congregations gave next to no support to synods; they in turn gave even less help to the work of the church-at-large. "Herr Pastor" often ruled with an iron hand as the undisputed leader of his own little personality cult. If a congregation did not like a particular action or program of the synod, it simply quit. The sectarian novelty of "congregational autonomy" was uncritically absorbed from the new religious culture, as cell after cell of unaffiliated Lutherans practiced a policy of "live and let live," and even "die and let die."

At the same time, the Lutheran confessional concern, when confronted with all kinds of liberal teachings and unevangelical sects, often hardened into a very unlovely type of *dogmatism*. Faith in God became virtually identical with beliefs about God. A rock-ribbed biblicism became far more interested in exposing how Lutherans differed from Calvinists and Roman Catholics than in revealing how they compared with Jesus Christ. A rigid scholasticism led some Lutherans to deny pulpit and altar fellowship to some of their less narrow fellow confessionalists. A legalistic moralism prompted the cutting of still more ties with brothers and sisters in Christ over minor disputes on adiaphorous matters which the church had formerly left to Christian freedom.

Finally, the Lutheran liturgy, particularly in foreign languages, often contributed to their cultic and communal *isolationism*. As foreigners, Lutherans were often looked upon with suspicion, especially since their doctrinal position apparently forbade them to engage in very much common worship or work with fellow-Christians. Indeed, Protestants of the Free Church tradition generally considered Lutherans to be "half-Catholic," because of their formal liturgical worship and general distrust of religious revivalism and moralistic crusades. In short, liturgy also helped to erect and perpetuate the barriers between Lutherans and the Puritanical and revivalistic religious culture in the United States.

Official relationships with non-Lutherans slowly came to be governed by two guidelines commonly called the "evangelical" and "representative" principles.[8] We agreed to relate only to agencies that were composed exclusively of churches which confessed the lordship of Jesus Christ. We also insisted that accountable representatives of our church sit only with their official counterparts from other church bodies, not with persons who represented only themselves or nonconfessional agencies. Since this twofold polciy allowed no openings for association with nonchurch agencies, it served only to reenforce Lutheran community isolation.

Against this background, it was considered only natural for the Lutheran Church in America's "Commission on the Nature and Mission of the Congregation" (1966) to include in its Manifesto to each congregation a call "to engage in co-operative action with neighboring congregations and councils of churches which with it confess Jesus Christ as divine Lord and Savior" (#5).

What represented a major breakthrough in that convention-approved Manifesto, though, were the three subsequent appeals:

8. Further documentation is provided in the parish study guide of my *In, Not Of; Living Our Baptism in the World* (Philadelphia: Lutheran Church Press, 1974), pp. 99–101.

To be alert to the changing needs, moods, and currents of the modern world in order to fulfill its ministry more effectively [#6];

To adapt its methods and programs to the specific community or communities which it is called to serve, recognizing especially the dramatic increase in the proportion of youth in the general population [#7]; and

To lift its voice in concord and to work in concert with forces for good, cooperating with church and other groups participating in activities that promote justice, relieve misery, and reconcile the estranged (#8).

Although that action represented a dramatic change in the corporate pieties of all the predecessor bodies of the Lutheran Church in America (LCA), it was thoroughly grounded in Lutheran confessional theology. The Augsburg Confession had always clearly recognized both "Christian righteousness" and "civil righteousness." The former relates to God's "right-hand" rule through the gospel: the personal salvation of Christians "by grace, for Christ's sake, through faith" (Article IV). The latter relates to God's "left-hand" rule through the law: the social morality by which all persons created in God's image, Christians and non-Christians alike, are able "to live an outwardly honorable life and to make choices among the things that reason comprehends" (Article XVIII). Assertion #8 of the Manifesto simply championed twentieth century civil righteousness.

The Lutheran Church in America has since made these principles a part of the church's constitution. Any of its congregations or agencies "in obedience to their Lord and motivated by Christian love, may cooperate in community action organizations with other religious bodies and/or other civic-minded groups, both voluntary and governmental, in endeavors to effect changes in the social order designed to permeate society with justice."

Moreover, to facilitate maximal Lutheran involvement in community affairs, LCA policymakers have declared that "neither the evangelical nor the representative principle need apply when such cooperation focuses essentially on promoting justice, relieving misery, and reconciling the estranged."

This whole development represents a watershed in the maturation of American Lutheranism. The events of World War II, the decline of the number of European immigrants, and the societal eruptions of the 1960s, all combined to crack open the hard shell of Lutheran isolationism. Assertion #8 of the Manifesto was a public declaration that American Lutheranism had finally recovered its justice-oriented integrity in civil relationships. Although it had developed largely as an ethnic ghetto, it was now venturing forth as the servant church of the Servant Lord. Lutherans were affirming that "living their Baptism" means to carry out God's whole mission in and for the world as baptized servants who embody the compassion of Christ.

Each congregation now bears responsibility for developing and maintaining an effective Christian witness for justice in the neighborhood or community in which it is geographically located. The particular forms in which this witness can best express itself can be determined only after careful study. Pastors and members will need to evaluate the human and social needs of the neighborhood and the resources which may be available to the congregation.

Attention should center both on preventive action and on remedial care in addressing social ills. Community social action organizations, social service agencies and institutions, and governmental programs in health, education, and welfare, all represent potential allies for the congregation in its service to the communtiy. Therefore, the church now gladly joins with other forces in achieving social change for justice and reconciliation in society. Individuals are enabled to grow, to gain new dignity, and to become effective participants in the decision-making process which affects their own lives. People come closer to developing fully the potential which the Creator has placed in every human being.

In light of the total American Lutheran experience, however, this gradual recovery of an essential part of the church's total ministry is very spotty in different parts of the country. Generally speaking, some of the strongest resistance to the struggle for more social justice comes from those local congregations which stubbornly refuse to engage in any corporate planning or cooperative programs for community service. No matter what the cost, they want to "go it alone."

Furthermore, they often justify their rejection of offers of outside help from synodical officials or specialists on boards and agencies of the church-at-large by an appeal to the alleged sanctity of their "congregational autonomy." However over-simplified our description, this situation poses a very serious problem for the social responsibility of the Lutheran Church in our day.

Our next task is to provide the theological criteria by which we may judge the validity of this kind of response, and to suggest the general direction in which the church should move in meeting more adequately its total calling under God.[9] To develop the normative Lutheran view of the church's nature, mission, and structure, we shall concentrate on those salient features of Article VII of the Augsburg Confession which help to explain the four classical marks of the church confessed in the Nicene Creed.

> Our churches also teach that one holy church is to continue forever. The church is the assembly of saints in which the Gospel is taught purely and the sacraments are administered rightly. For the true unity of the church, it is enough to agree concerning the teaching of the Gospel and the administration of the sacraments. It is not necessary that human traditions or rites and ceremonies, instituted by men, should be alike everywhere. It is as Paul says, "One faith, one baptism, one God and Father of all" (Eph. 4:5, 6).

The Church's Function and Structure

1. The church is *apostolic*; it is constituted by the apostolic message, as it is proclaimed in word and sacrament.

It is of the greatest importance that Article VII describes the church dynamically and functionally in terms of what is actually happening within it. The church derives its apostolic authority from its faithful conformity to, and transmission of, the apos-

9. This doctrine of the church is amplified in the final chapters of my *Helping Youth and Adults Know Doctrine,* (Philadelphia: Lutheran Church Press, 1963).

tolic gospel. The good news of God's mighty act in Christ for the salvation of a fallen mankind either makes or breaks the church as the church. It is to be identified by faith, and not by sight, wherever and whenever the events of God's self-revelation take place. As long as our proclamation of the gospel is in essential agreement with the apostolic gospel, we may be certain that the church is present which Christ himself instituted and which he commissioned the apostles to spread over the face of the earth.

The church is continually in danger of interpreting its means of grace in an impersonal, mechanical fashion. Jesus Christ, the living Word of God, employs these sanctified channels in order to give himself to his beloved. It is not something, but someone, who is really present under the "masks" of creation, whenever "the gospel is rightly preached and the sacraments rightly administered." In Christian worship, therefore, it is Christ who acts and we who respond. It is he who first offers to us the free and undeserved forgiveness of our sin. This then engenders and empowers our faithful response of prayer, praise, and thanksgiving.

Once this Christ-centered testimony of the apostles is properly understood, there can be no more human-centered talk of "autonomy," whether of the local congregation or any other part of Christ's church. In the body of Christ, all members suffer and rejoice together once autonomy (self-rule) has been replaced by theonomy (God-rule). The church is not the subject but the object of the love of God. The church does not constitute God's Word; the Word of God constitutes the church.

In terms of the church's structure, this means that no group of Christians, whether in a local congregation or a larger body, can think of itself in selfish isolation. More specifically, no local congregation, by virtue of an unevangelical view of its alleged "autonomy," may properly engage in any action (or inaction) which tends to destroy the apostolicity of the very Word which sustains it. Such community-disregarding individualism is often the bane of all congregational forms of polity.

2. The church is *catholic*; it is the communion of saints, the

whole people of God throughout all history and eternity.

In the Formula of Concord, "catholic" is replaced by "Christian" so as to emphasize the true nature of the church's catholicity. Here there is no thought of any quantitative, geographical universality. It is rather an evangelical confession in the qualitative, redemptive universality of Christ's mission and message. It is the Christ-centered message, and not the messengers, which constitutes the church's apostolicity. So it is also the reigning Christ, and not the sacerdotal hierarchy, which marks the church's catholicity.

The church is composed of "saints." These are children of God whom the Holy Spirit has "called, gathered and enlightened" through the saving proclamation of the gospel. These are the forgiven sinners who truly believe that Jesus Christ is Lord and who trust in him for their eternal salvation. Where Christ is, there is also the church.

Despite its incarnate Lord, the church has often hesitated when it comes to affirming the inseparable unity of the universal and the particular within the local congregation of believers. Sometimes it has denied that all baptized Christians are saints, reserving that designation for a spiritual elite who have achieved some special piety or outstanding works. The New Testament is clear, however, in addressing all believing Christians as "saints." They are the elect of God—whatever their persisting shortcomings—whom the Holy Spirit has set apart in consecrated discipleship.

In like fashion, the church's disdain for particularity has often been exhibited by a geographical interpretation of its catholicity. This must also be repudiated. The church's catholicity consists in the universality of Christ's redeeming work. Since Christ is redemptively at work wherever the gospel is rightly proclaimed, then it follows, paradoxically, that the church has no more catholic expression on earth than in the worship life of the local congregation. It is not in the administrative programs of the church headquarters, but in the local assembly of believers that we join "with angels and archangels and with all the company of heaven" in praising God's glorious Name.

The church must be on its guard against the perennial lure of clericalism. Christians conformed to Christ are to serve, not to be served (heteronomy). When related to church structure, this means that the integrity and sanctity of every congregational ministry—whatever its persisting shortcomings—must be recognized and respected by all jurisdictional units of the church at large. Not to do this is a particularly dangerous temptation in all episcopal forms of polity.

3. The church is *holy*; it is the community of faith and love in which the Holy Spirit grants persons the pardon for their salvation and the power for their service.

Once again, the peculiarity of an evangelical ecclesiology is in its confession that the church's holiness consists solely in Christ, its gracious Head, and not in any perfection of its members. The Christian's whole life is one of continual repentance, daily death, and rebirth. We are declared righteous by a gracious God for Christ's sake alone. Our sanctification remains a lifelong process of being restored by the indwelling Holy Spirit to the loving image of God in which we were created. Sin persists in the heart of every redeemed person. At once righteous and sinful, Christians are in continual need of the saving Word of God both to bolster our faith and to fire our love.

The holy self-sacrifice of Christ is alone acceptable in God's sight as an expiation for human sin. Therefore, Holy Scripture declares Christ to be the church's only Mediator and true High Priest. The atonement of the sinless Son of God at Calvary is the only sacrifice in which Christians can safely put their trust. Christ's saving righteousness is reckoned to all who believed in him. Before God, no further human sacrifices are either necessary or desired. In the new testament established by Christ, all baptized Christians are incorporated into "a chosen race, a royal priesthood, a holy nation, God's own people."

Conformed to the shape of their divine Head, all members of the body of Christ are likewise declared to be "kings and priests." They are to offer themselves as "living sacrifices" in obedient faith toward God and in loving service to other persons. In this universal priesthood of believers, some will exercise their callings in the forms of a public ministry of word and sacrament in the church. Others, recognizing that all neighbor-serving occupations are equal in God's sight, will work to God's glory in domestic and secular pursuits.

Crucial for us is the conclusion that a church's polity should be of such a character that it encourages all Christians to assume the many societal responsibilities inherent in the priesthood of all believers. Our church insists that there is only a functional difference of services between the clergy and the laity. Lutherans must therefore be careful to employ only those organizational forms and structures which afford all Christians the opportunity for the full exercise of their lay ministries.

4. The church is *one*; it has one faith, one baptism, one Lord, one God and Father of us all. Though essentially one, however, the church is both a religious organism and a social organization. As the body of Christ it can only be believed; as the Lutheran Church in America it may be structured with any polity which does not belie its nature or thwart its mission.

On the one hand, the church is an eschatological community of grace which, like its members, is "in" but "not of" this world. It is the cosmic fellowship of all those in heaven and on earth who confess Jesus Christ as Lord and Savior. In essence it is a spiritual fellowship of all those who have lived in true faith, hope, and love under God.

On the other hand, this eternal *Una Sancta* manifests itself historically through public communities of organized Christians gathered about the Word of God. Wheat and chaff continue to coexist in the institutional church. Nevertheless, Scripture assures us that Christ himself is really present in the church's means of grace in order to incorporate men into God's eternal kingdom. As God became incarnate in the man Jesus, the kingdom of God takes on tangible form in the ecclesiastical institution. And as there is only one Lord, so too there is only one church. Yet without falling into any kind of Platonic dualism, we must always clearly distinguish the eternal and the temporal dimensions of this one holy church which will last forever.

Furthermore, the Lutheran confessions are unanimous in

142

affirming that church structure is a matter of adiaphorous Christian freedom. For the unity of the church, "it is enough to agree concerning the teaching of the Gospel and the administration of the sacraments" (Augsburg Confession, Article VII). The church is Christ's body and not ours. All of our human traditions (rites, ceremonies, and polities) are theologically neutral. They are good and useful if they help us to transmit the saving gospel; they are evil and even idolatrous if they stand in its way.

God leaves it to the consecrated reason and common sense of his faithful to use whatever form of polity most effectively implements the church's ministry of reconciliation at any given time and place. Polities may freely be changed to meet changing times and needs; only the gospel must remain the same.

In the course of our theological analysis we have arrived at three general guideposts which should provide normative direction (rather than legislation) for the problem of church structures:

(1) No congregation should act so autonomously that it destroys the church's apostolicity;

(2) No church body should act so heteronomously that it destroys the congregation's catholicity;

(3) Any polity may be employed by the Lutheran church which expedites the proclamation of the gospel and which implements the exercise of the priesthood of all believers.

The Church's Objectives and Administration

Too many Lutherans are still committed to "organizational Pietism." This is the simplistic and naive view that "function" is of God and "structure" is of Satan, and never the twain shall meet in the institutional church.

We need to gain a lot more clarity on our theology of church administration. The societal struggle between Lutheran quietists and activists in the 1960s has now been institutionally internalized in the ecclesiastical tension between Pietists and planners in the 1970s. As personal love was then pitted against social justice, it is now being cast against corporate efficiency. Now as then, liberals and conservatives alike are making an "either-or" out of a "both-and" to our mutual detriment.

The unresolved theological issue is virtually identical in both decades. It is the perennial temptation of that Lutheran dualism in totally severing the realms of the law and the gospel, the realms of the secular and the sacred in God's double reign as our Creator and Redeemer.

1. *God's gospel governs the faith of the administrator, while the inseparable works of his administration remain under God's law.*

We may illustrate this thesis with a picturesque quote from Luther in which he reminds us that the first Christmas shepherds returned not to a monastery, but to their sheep, after they had seen the Christ-child. It portrays the truth that coming to know and love Christ does not necessarily change what we do, but rather why, and how, and for whom we do it.

> Christian freedom is not bound to any particular work, for all works which come along are of equal worth to a Christian. The shepherds did not run off to the desert, don cowls, shave their heads, or change any of their external practices in clothing, time, food, or drink. They returned instead to serve God by caring for their flocks. For Christian faith does not consist in external activities which man has to change, but in an inward transformation by which he receives a new heart, spirit, will, and disposition. He does exactly the same external works as his neighbor who has no faith. A Christian knows that everything depends upon faith alone, and he is free to go, stay, eat, drink, work, or live as other men in public office and estates without anyone ever knowing of his Christianity. (*WA* 10, 1, 1, 137)

Even the most cursory reading of Luther reveals a surprising number of references to the distinction between God's twofold rule as Creator and Redeemer by law and gospel. We repeat, for emphasis, the admirably high position which Luther affords to human reason when it is properly employed in the service of neighbors and limited to managing the technical affairs of every-day life. In the realm of redemption, reason is a "whore" if it seduces us away from scriptural revelation. In the realm of creation, however, reason can be the servant of love in achieving human justice.

> God has placed man's civil life under the dominion of natural reason which has ability enough to rule physical things. Reason and experience together teach man how to govern his wife and family, how to care for his livestock, and how to do everything else that belongs to sustaining a life here on earth. These powers have been graciously bestowed by God upon man's reason, and we do not need to look to Scripture for advice in such temporal matters. God has seen to it that even the heathen is blessed with the gift of reason to help him live his daily life. (*WA* 16, 353)

2. *The institutional church is a secular reality under the law of God the Creator, while the one, holy, catholic and apostolic church is an inseparable spiritual reality under the gospel of God the Redeemer.*

Luther's clear distinction—without separation or identification—between a person's faith (as a gospel-governed Christian) and his reason (as a law-governed creature) is carried through consistently in his view of the institutional church as a secular reality, and of church polity as adiaphorous to salvation. For Luther and the Lutheran confessions, the institutional church is always treated—though far too infrequently!—as an "external, temporal thing."

Too often today, Lutherans tend to identify the realm of creation and its secular authority with the institutional state, and the realm of redemption and its spiritual authority with the institutional church. Yet that denies our confessed theology that the church—as its crucified and risen Lord—is both divine and human, both a spiritual organism (the body of Christ) and a secular organization (the Lutheran Church in America).

So, for example, many Lutherans turn instinctively to the Small Catechism's treatment of the third article of the Apostles' Creed, when they look for Luther's interpretation of the church. Yet there is not one word about the *institutional* church in that familiar place. Rather Lutherans proclaim there the work of the Holy Spirit as believed from above ("the one holy Christian church on earth") and as believed from below ("the communion of saints" as a spiritual fellowship).

To get any word from Luther's catechism on the institutional church, we must turn rather to the section on the law of the Ten Commandments. Moreover, in his explanation of the Ten Commandments in the Large Catechism, Luther also discerningly treats the church's dual nature in two different places. First, the redemptive power of God in the one, holy, catholic, and apostolic church is developed under the first commandment: "You shall have no other gods." Second, the nonredemptive authority of the institutional church is developed under the fourth commandment: "You shall honor your father and mother." In short, the administration of the institutional church is analyzed by Luther as an extension of parental authority under the second table of God's law.

How Luther justified that "extension"—in opposition to Rome's claim that a particular form of church government is divinely ordained—is of great interest to us. In providing the Small Catechism's meaning of "Honor your father and mother" for baptized Christians, Luther answers: "We should fear and love God, and so we should not despise our parents *and superiors* [*sic*!], not provoke them to anger, but honor, serve, obey, love, and esteem them" (Tappert, ed., *Book of Concord*, 343).

Note well Luther's exegetical expansion of "parents" to include the new phrase: "and superiors." In Luther's explanatory material on the fourth commandment in the Large Catechism, the issue of church government and its administration is thereby indirectly introduced through that side door.

> Thus far we have three kinds of fathers presented in this commandment: fathers by blood, fathers of a household, and fathers of a nation. Besides these, there are also spiritual fathers—not like those in the papacy who applied this title to themselves but performed no fatherly office. For the name spiritual father belongs only to those who govern and guide us by the Word of God. . . . Although the duty of superiors is not explicitly stated in the Ten Commandments [*sic!*], it is frequently dealt with in many other passages of Scripture, and God intends it to be included in this commandment in which he speaks of father and mother. God

146

does not want to have knaves or tyrants in this office and respon- sibility; nor does he assign them this honor (that is, power and authority to govern) merely to receive homage. . . . Therefore do not imagine that the [parental] office is a matter of your pleasure and whim. It is a strict commandment and injunction of God who holds you accountable for it. (*BC*, 387–388)

This rather casual treatment of church polity and adminis- tration helps to underscore the theological, rather than political, center of gravity for the Reformation. Luther had little interest or gift for administration. (That's why Katie ran the family budget in the Black Cloister after their marriage!)

The Augsburg Confession is satisfied to limit itself to the negative assertion that church administration—together with other man-made ceremonies and arrangements—has·nothing to do with the certainty of our eternal salvation (Article VII). Lutherans have had to learn the hard way—down to our own day—the corollary truth that church administration still has a lot to do with the effectiveness of our temporal service.

3. *The biblical and theological answer is that church adminis- tration is not directly a biblical or theological question.*

Exegetically, "administration" is normally rooted in exercis- ing ministry or service (*diakonia,* e.g., 1 Cor. 12:5; 2 Cor. 9:12). In the New Testament, understandably, administration has nothing to do with our modern notions of the executive management of the organizational structures of the institutional church. This is also true of the oft-misused passage, 1 Cor. 12:28 (citing "administrators" between "healers" and "speakers in various kinds of tongues") in the list of the Holy Spirit's diverse gifts and functions. Indeed, in the earliest cited examples of such "administrative" activity, the seven Hellenists ("deacons") assumed responsibility for administering meals for the needy and engaging in charity work (Acts 6:2–6).

It is therefore wholly anachronistic and exegetically illegiti- mate to seek any biblicistic solutions to problems of modern church administration. These problems arose in the embryonic beginnings of their present forms only centuries after the delayed return of the risen Christ and the compilation of the Holy

147

Scriptures. We conclude that the biblical answer is that church administration is not directly a biblical question.

Theologically, the Pauline distinction between the law and the gospel in the realms of creation and redemption helps us to understand the proper relation of the Holy Spirit to the church of Jesus Christ, along with its means of grace and need for organizational administration.

Administration involves the rational management of power (persons, processes) to achieve certain goals. It is a secular function performed under God's law of creation. It is part of our responsible stewardship of the gifts of the Creator, not of the Spirit, even when exercised in the just and efficient management of the institutional church ("earthen vessel"). Unlike the word and the sacraments, which constitute the one, holy, catholic, and apostolic church "in, with and under" the Lutheran Church of America, administration is not a constitutive mark of the church. It is not a means of grace through which the Holy Spirit conveys the real presence and benefits of the risen Christ among us. Hence there is no such thing as "Christian" administration (any more than "Christian" plumbing or baking). There are rather baptized Christians who rationally administer, plumb, and bake—to God's glory.

However, the story is very different regarding the *persons* who serve as church administrators. Empowered as temples of God's Holy Spirit, Christians who administer are often "called, enlightened and sanctified" to propose and implement objectives that are distinctly informed by Christian theology. It is intrinsic to their growth in grace under God's gospel of redemption. Church administrators may, therefore, pursue policies that are just and equitable to God's children, and implement objectives that witness loyally to God's kingdom.

Church administrators, empowered by the Spirit, may engage in tasks that are highly beneficial (*bene esse*), even though not essential (*esse*), to the earthly mission of the church. They do so in living testimony to the incarnational character of Christianity. Just as we certainly encounter God in the servant-form of Jesus of Nazareth, so we are certainly incorporated into the kingdom of God in the servant-form of the administered congregations and organized synods of the institutional church. In God's incarnational strategy, the finite conveys the infinite (*"Finitum capax infiniti"*).

On the one hand, then, Lutherans do not attempt to sacralize or transform in substance (transubtantiate) the secular skills of administration into a saving means of grace. On the other hand, however, Lutheran churchmen should view their call to administer as an occupation of service worthy of their Christian vocation. We conclude, in parallel fashion, that the theological answer is likewise that church administration is not directly a theological question.

We may summarize all that has been said with a simple theological formula: *As the gospel determines the "who" and "why" of the church administrator, so the law governs the inseparable "how" and "what" of church administration.*

Lutherans confess that God's Word is composed of the law and the gospel. The *gospel* has both a theological function (to grant faith) and an ethical function (to inspire love). So, too, the *law* has both a theological function (to condemn sin) and a civil function (to promote justice).

Consequently, (1) the gospel's *theological* function addresses the "who," the administrator himself, the person behind the office title who faithfully accepts God's grace in Christ through the power of the Spirit. (2) The gospel's *ethical* function relates to the "why," to the administrator's motivation, the responsible attempt to put his faith to work in love as he expresses his Christian vocation (in baptism) through his ecclesiastical occupation (as a church leader).

In corollary fashion, (1) the law's *theological* function relates to the "how," to the corporate life-style of the organization, accusing it of sin wherever it attempts to deify itself (in efficient but demonic objectives), or to dehumanize its workers or constituents (in pragmatic but degrading policies). (2) The law's *civil* function relates to the "what," to the programs and operations of the organization, measuring their effectiveness in employing faith-activated love to balance the counterclaims of

149

reason and power to achieve the highest levels of production and justice that are reasonably attainable.

Finally, there is continual and dynamic interaction between law and gospel, administration and administrator, sin and grace. Tensions abound. This underscores the reality that church administration when performed at its best remains a personal art, rather than an impersonal science.

For example, PPBS stands for "program, planning, budget systems" when performed by any rational person. But when performed by a conscientious Christian, PPBS will also stand for pain, patience, bravery, and suffering. Why?—because beloved children of God are affected by every difficult decision made by a church executive as a conscientious steward of the "power of God unto service."

The conclusion is that all administration, including the administration of the institutional church, is ordained by God to remain secular and to enjoy a *relative* autonomy of its own under God's sovereign law. (To put it boldly, $2 and $2 are $4, and 2 acres and 2 acres are 4 acres, whether or not Jesus rose from the dead.) Hence it is not faith, hope, and charity, but rather reason, power, and justice that are regulative for the temporal realms of life, including the administration and planning of the Lutheran Church in America.

At the same time, however, even though there are no "Christian" organizations, the institutional church is nevertheless an organization of Christians. It is a committed fellowship of baptized persons that may be blessed by God with the distinctiveness of *theologically informed objectives and pastorally concerned policies.*

We should be able to demonstrate some tangible differences as we use, modify, or replace PPBS or any other management system in our attempts to put priorities on our money, time, and talents for the mission of God's kingdom. Our calling is to be faithful, whether or not we are successful. "Seek ye first the kingdom of God and his righteousness" is not merely a pious platitude. It is a normative objective to which faithful and rational Christians who administer and plan can attach some fairly realistic aims, flexible programs, and supportive funds. (That is, *since* Jesus rose from the dead, $4 and 4 acres are also viewed by the faithful Christian as potential resources for the growth of God's kingdom, transcending the economic facts of life.)

Lutheran theology supports the biblical view that church administration—like the Sabbath—is made for persons, and persons are made for God. Jesus Christ is Lord, and the church's faith must govern its institutional structures and programs. Church management is responsible stewardship. Where Christians are illumined and empowered by the Holy Spirit, faith can illumine reason, love can temper justice, and hope can generate power. This is God's promise whenever baptized Christians meet their administrative responsibilities as part of their Christian discipleship.

LUTHERANS INVOLVED IN JUSTICE

In the Fourth Gospel, Jesus speaks these words to God the Father: "I do not pray that thou shouldst take them out of the world, but that thou shouldst keep them from the evil one. They are not of the world, even as I am not of the world. Sanctify them in the truth; thy word is truth. As thou didst send me into the world, so I have sent them into thy world" (John 17:15–18).

This petition helps Christians to understand the peculiar interaction of discipleship and citizenship. On the one hand, "they are not of the world." Christians are a holy people, disciples whom God calls to be citizens in Christ's eternal kingdom of faith and love. On the other hand, "I have sent them into the world." Christians are also a secular people, witnesses whom God calls to be citizens in Caesar's temporal kingdom of law and justice.

We confess that God remains the sole Lord of life, whether he rules persons as saints through Christ and the church or as citizens through Caesar and the state. Consequently, our chief task in this chapter is to reaffirm the "sacred secularity" of God's people as they worship, witness, and work in his world.[10]

Sacred Secularity

It is crucial that Christian citizens distinguish their sacred secularity from godless secularism. Christ wants his people to be "in" but "not of" this world. The temptation is to be of this world while in it. Christians are not to be the same as other human creatures of God with whom they are called to identify. Through their sacred secularity, they become the "light" which illumines, the "yeast" which transforms, and the "salt" which flavors the world in which Christ lived and for which he died (Matt. 5:13–16). As his living body, the church, Christians participate in Christ's ongoing ministry in and for the world.

In terms of this study, *secularity* means rendering to Caesar the things that are Caesar's, whereas *secularism* means rendering to Caesar the things that are God's. Secularity reflects a God-centered faith. It views the state as free from the domination of the church but still subject to the sovereign will of God. St. Paul teaches that civil authorities are "ministers of God" (Rom. 13:6). They are officeholders through whom God rules the temporal affairs of his children. It is to God's universal law that politicians and statesmen are ultimately accountable.

By contrast, secularism expresses a human-centered faith. It views the state as free from both the church and the will of God in its own sovereign autonomy. In its democratic form, secularism disregards the lordship of God and asserts that "the voice of the people is the voice of God." Far worse, the fascist motto says: "Everything for the state; nothing against the state; nothing outside the state." This reveals how idolatrous secularism can become under a dictatorship.

10. This chapter is based on an updated revision of my contribution to an interdisciplinary symposium supporting *Church and State; a Lutheran Perspective,* a social statement adopted by the Third Biennial Convention of the binational Lutheran Church in America, Kansas City, Missouri, June 21–29, 1966.

The responsible citizenship of Christians is therefore one of God's most effective weapons against the state's self-worship. Government leaders undergo intense temptations to evil (witness the Watergate scandals). The demonic potentialities within any government inspired Luther's famous warning, "A wise prince is a rare bird in heaven, still more a pious prince." Yet the tragic fact is that too many German Lutherans betrayed Luther's biblical realism in the 1930s by capitulating to Nazism. That makes it all the more urgent for American Lutherans to testify boldly to the true function of the secular state as a servant of God.

Previous chapters have given biblical and theological grounds for rejecting the two most obvious approaches to the American church-state dilemma. (By "state" we denote the politically organized community with its monopoly of coercive power. By "church" we refer here loosely to the plurality of voluntary religious associations dependent on noncoercive motivation and persuasion.)

At one extreme, there is no desire to have the state control the church. This dates all the way back to the warning of the apostles to all potential dictators. They said, "We must obey God rather than men" (Acts 5:29), whenever the integrity of the church's proclamation is endangered. American Christians may, therefore, be grateful that the First Amendment to the United States Constitution guarantees the "free exercise" of religion to all its citizens.

At the other extreme, we do not want to move toward church control of the state. "My kingship is not of this world" (John 18:36), Christ warns those contemporary zealots who believe that America could or should be legislated into a "Christian" nation. Again the Christian may be thankful that the First Amendment also prohibits Congress from making any law "respecting an establishment of religion" in the United States. In short, neither a state-controlled church nor a church-controlled state should be advocated by North American Christians.

A growing number of political controversies with religious overtones is encouraging many insecure Christians in America

153

to endorse Jefferson's personal (nonconstitutional) hope for an absolute "wall of separation" between church and state. As a religious deist who rejected the inbreaking kingdom of God, Jefferson advocated absolute separation as the best pattern for the protection of religious liberty and the avoidance of civil strife (see *Everson v. Board of Education,* 1952). For these "strict separationists," Americans must now quickly repair the many holes that past generations have permitted in the mythical wall separating the realms of the "sacred" and the "secular."

The biblical view of the sacredness of secular life leads us to reject this extreme position of an *absolute* separation of church and state. We dare never forget—nor let others forget—that the same God is Lord of the nations as well as Head of the church. By clearly distinguishing God's law of creation from his gospel of redemption, the Reformers found a way by which church and state could interact without being united and yet remain distinct without being divorced.

Christians should never scorn "the secular" as being godless or profane. *Saeculum* is the Latin equivalent of the Greek word in the New Testament which refers to this age, to humanity's temporal, earthly life. In praise of God the Creator, Christians should welcome the secular or civil dimensions of this world. "Since the time of the apostles," boasted Luther, "the temporal sword and temporal government have not been so clearly described or so highly praised as by me." The secular realm, though not redemptive, is still a sacred reality of God's creation. It provides many of the "masks" through which God graciously preserves the world from its sinful self-destruction.

To put it as sharply as possible, the state cannot be too secular (civil) from the Christian point of view! Our initial shock at such a statement reveals the need to replace political rhetoric with theological clarity.

We shall defend both an institutional separation and a functional interaction of church and state in the United States and Canada. This position is determined by our fidelity to the Christian view of history. We believe that Jesus Christ has inaugurated but not yet consummated the kingly rule of God in the midst of the secular kingdoms of this world. During the present age, both the church and the state are divinely commissioned to play their distinct but related roles in God's preservation and salvation of mankind.

Church and State: (1) Institutional Separation

We turn first to support America's institutional separation of church and state. According to the Lutheran confessions, church polity is a matter which Christians may structure in any beneficial way according to the demands and opportunities of local conditions.

Lutherans in Germany and Scandinavia usually developed a pattern of established "folk churches" after the Reformation. However, this arrangement was possible only because of the religious and cultural unity which prevailed among them. Even so, the obvious advantages in being able to expose a whole people to the Christian message and ethos were frequently offset by weaknesses in bureaucracy and traditionalism. In view of the religious and cultural pluralism which has always prevailed among American colonists and immigrants, our institutional separation of church and state appears to be the most equitable arrangement. This system guarantees each institution the freedom to perform its own God-ordained tasks for the common good.

What is the nature and mission of the church under God? For our purposes, the church's nature can be summarized in the classical marks confessed in the Nicene Creed. The church is "one." It is the family of God in which persons called by the Holy Spirit share one Lord, one faith, and one baptism. The church is "holy." It is the communion of saints in which people empowered by the Holy Spirit are sanctified by grace through love and hope. The church is "catholic." It is the universal body of Christ in which persons enlightened by the Holy Spirit are justified by grace through faith. The church is "apostolic." It is the assembly of believers in which people are gathered by the Holy Spirit through the proclamation of the apostolic message in speech and action.

155

This one, holy, catholic, and apostolic church manifests itself in the world through public communities of organized Christian believers. The church militant is therefore both a divine organism related to Christ and a human organization related to the state. As an ecclesiastical institution, its distinctive mission is to proclaim the Word of God in preaching and sacraments, worship and evangelism, educational and social ministry.

First, the church proclaims God's Word through preaching and sacraments. The risen Lord is present to bless his repentant and faithful people wherever the commands and promises of God are rightly preached and the sacraments are rightly administered. Through these channels, Christ bestows his gifts of pardon for our rebellion and power for our renewal. By the inner testimony of the Holy Spirit, an evangelical sermon confronts the hearer with God's Word as a personal message of judgment and mercy. Furthermore, as effectual signs of God's kingdom among us, evangelical sacraments actually give what they signify through the presence of God's Word: forgiveness of sin, life, and salvation.

Second, the church witnesses to God's Word through its worship and evangelism. Christians have always felt constrained to worship God in prayer, praise, and thanksgiving. They do so in gratitude for the undeserved goodness of God, as revealed supremely in the person and work of Jesus Christ. Worship involves a gracious encounter between God and persons which issues in witness to their neighbors. First God offers them the saving benefits of Christ's victory over the forces of sin, death, and the demonic. Then they are empowered by God's Spirit to trust in his promises and to tell others the goods news that God in Christ is for us. Worship and evangelism become inseparable in daily life as Christians accept God's call to call others to discipleship.

Third, the church witnesses to God's Word through its educational and social ministry. Christians believe in a living God who acts in history. We treasure the Bible as the norm for Christian faith and life because it is the authoritative witness to and instrument of these mighty deeds of God for human salvation. Educational ministry in Bible and doctrine is therefore imperative for the church as it teaches its youth, instructs its converts, trains its clergy, and defends its faith against attack and error. In like fashion, Christians who have experienced the sacrificial love of God in their own lives will try to act lovingly to their neighbors. Through their works of mercy and struggles for justice, Christians witness in action to the loving and righteous Lord of history.

All this the church may do in America without hindrance or fear. Simultaneously, the institutional separation of church and state in the United States and Canada also permits the state to carry out its distinctive work without interference from the church. This now leads us to examine the *nature and mission of the state under God*.

The Christian view of the state is determined by a biblical realism which keeps Romans 13 and Revelation 13 in healthy tension. If Romans describes the divine side of the state, Revelation points out some of its more demonic features. The same Roman government which Paul lauds as a "minister of God" is denounced by the Seer John as a "beast" which blasphemes against God, makes war on his saints, and engages in imperialism against other nations. In brief, the state's God-ordained secularity in principle is continually in danger of succumbing to godless secularism in practice.

The state ("civil authority") is depicted in the New Testament as a divinely ordained institution. This does not mean that every particular government or governor enjoys God's personal stamp of approval. Far from it. It means rather that the state's "governing authority," as such, is to be respected and obeyed as an expression of the sovereign will of the Creator. In other words, Christians are not anarchists. They welcome civil authority as one of the "orders of preservation" through which God checks men's sinful injustice and encourages their mutual service.

The state's power is delegated to it by God. The government

is accountable to God for the ways in which it uses, abuses, or neglects to use its powerful civil "sword." This means, realistically, that the backbone of every state is might. Whether employed by Satan or against him, all politics is "power politics"—all unbiblical sentimentality notwithstanding.

However, this in no way justifies any state's self-deification. The state's power is not inherent. It is delegated by God to be used responsibly for the attainment of beneficial civil goals. This means that no state is worthy of the Christian's uncritical loyalty and unquestioning obedience. The state is in continual need of the prophetic guidance and judgment of the law of God—as proclaimed by the church—in order to be reminded of both its secular limits and potentialities.

The purpose of the state is to establish good order, peace and justice in a sinful world. In other words, its might must be enlisted in the service of right. But Christians should not expect love to replace justice in the operation of government. Civil authorities are not elected to run a pseudo-church on the basis of a culture-religion. The state's limited goal is earthly preservation under the law, not heavenly salvation under the gospel. Consequently, there is no "Christian" form of the state. While persons can be transformed by the gospel, institutions can only be reformed by the law. We can "Christianize" politicians and statesmen but not politics and the state. Impersonal institutions are ordained by God to remain secular. Hence, not faith and love but reason and justice are normative for the political realm. At the same time, faith can illumine reason and love can enlighten justice whenever Christian citizens meet their civil responsibilities.

In summary, the distinctive mission of the state is to establish civil justice through the maintenance of law and order, the protection of constitutional rights, and the promotion of the general welfare of the total citizenry.

First, the state establishes civil justice through the maintenance of law and order. Jefferson's beliefs that "the least government is the best government" and that "a revolution every twenty years is a good thing" find no support in Holy Scripture.

Before there can be any liberty and justice, there must be some law and order. This dare never be the government's last word, but it must be the first. As a restraining dike against sin, the state must be strong enough to compel its citizens' obedience to lawful authority in order to prevent mob-rule and anarchy. St. Paul teaches that civil authority is meant to be "a terror . . . to bad conduct" (Rom. 13:3). Evil persons should not be encouraged to engage in crime and corruption because the state is too weak to keep order and enforce laws.

Second, the state establishes civil justice through the protection of constitutional rights. This represents the other side of the coin in opposition to totalitarianism. As the government's power checks anarchy, so the citizens' rights hinder tyranny. Power often corrupts, and therefore government by law is far preferable to government by men. Under a dictatorial system, a single person, or a small elite can make or break "laws" at whim. People can be ruled by terror through the ruthless exercise of unchecked power. It is because of human sinfulness that Christians welcome a system of checks and balances in a constitutional democracy, where the government is forbidden to deprive any person of life, liberty, or property without due process of law.

Third, the state establishes civil justice through the promotion of the general welfare. It is now widely recognized that the modern state has a far more constructive role to play than merely wielding the "sword" against criminals and aggressors. It is also the task of a just government, in the interest of the common good, to guarantee equality of opportunity for the self-development of all citizens. Minority groups are in special need of governmental assistance and protection in such key areas as education, housing, employment, voting, and free access to public services and facilities. The state's responsibilities must now be vastly broadened under appropriate checks and balances. It must provide society the communal framework of justice within which all the other ordinances of God—home, school, work, recreation, etc.—can also perform their proper functions under God.

Church and State: (2) *Functional Interaction*

Americans and Canadians live in free lands which, while recognizing the institutional separation of church and state, nevertheless also favor a functional interaction which is mutually beneficial. This is as it should be. Jesus likened the kingdom of heaven to leaven (Matt. 13:33). The United States Supreme Court has said, "If a religious leaven is to be worked into the affairs of our people, it is to be done by individuals, groups, and churches, not by the government." Fair enough!

There has never really been an absolute "wall of separation" between church and state in either the United States or Canada. Despite Jefferson's private views, the First Amendment of the United States Constitution does not say that in every and all respects there needs to be complete separation. It is an historical fact that the government of the United States has generally been friendly toward religion while remaining officially neutral among the various religions. There are numerous ways without the risk of an official "establishment" by which the state, simply by fulfilling the duties of a just state, is thereby also helpful to the church. In the other direction, Americans have found many ways by which the church, solely through the "free exercise" of its divine mandate, is thereby also of help to the state. Let us examine five of the most important of these in turn.

First, the church relates to the interests of the state by offering intercessory prayers on its behalf. Christians are called to offer supplications and thanksgiving for all persons, especially "for kings and all who are in high positions." This intercession is vital because God is the author of all the power, wisdom, and courage needed for the government's successful operation. He alone is Lord of the state, even when unacknowledged, working order out of chaos, peace out of strife, and justice out of lawlessness. These divine blessings are also mutually beneficial because a just and effective state is able to preserve the kind of world in which the church can proclaim the Word of God.

Second, the church relates to the interests of the state by encouraging responsible citizenship and government service. The church has always admonished its members to be "subject to the governing authorities" out of respect for the civil power ordained by God. Just rulers can depend on the loyal support of Christian citizens. Unjust rulers may anticipate opposition. In such cases, it may become necessary for Christians as citizens to engage in civil disobedience or armed rebellion in selective conscientious opposition to an unjust government. Nevertheless, even then, such action is done in obedience to the God-ordained "civil authority" that is being violated by the unjust rulers in power. This same respect for the state is demonstrated when the church encourages qualified persons to enter some form of government service. In the conviction that there is only a difference of function between the ministries of the clergy and the laity, evangelical Christians look with great favor on these civil "ministers of God."

Third, the church relates to the interests of the state by holding it accountable to the sovereign law of God. Acting as "God's watchman," the church proclaims the general norms and guidelines of Christian political ethics in order to provide judgment and guidance for those leaders responsible under God for the peace, justice, and freedom of the world. The church must speak authoritatively for God, even though it cannot speak infallibly as God. The ethical and technical alternatives in a given situation may at times even be clear enough to justify a definite stand on a specific policy of the government in relation to a domestic or international issue. Unpopular as this may be, the church should fearlessly judge and arouse the conscience of the state in the name of the Lord of the nations.

Fourth, the church relates to the interests of the state by contributing to the civil consensus which supports it. The church strives to help create a moral and legal climate of opinion in which solutions to vexing political problems can take place more easily. In an age of corporate decision-making, the public witness of official representatives of the church-at-large can be particularly important in expressing the ethical judgments of the Christian community. Certain of the righteousness of God through faith in Jesus Christ, Christians are free both personally and corporately to join with other persons of good will—whatever their faith—in working for more just civil approximations of the moral law of God. Such cooperation is possible because some form of God's law (however corrupted by sin) is to be found written on the hearts of all persons (Romans 1–2). Through the insights of God's general revelation outside Holy Scripture, all rational persons can achieve a large measure of consensus on the state's function to establish an order of justice under the "laws of nature and nature's God" (Declaration of Independence).

Fifth, the church relates to the interests of the state by championing the human and civil rights of all its citizens. Christians believe that under God the state exists for people, not people for the state. The American Revolution was fought—and constitutional rights won—by persons who were willing to die for their belief that "governments are instituted among men, deriving their just powers from the consent of the governed" (Declaration of Independence). Yet the new nation then denied basic civil rights to over a million persons whose skin was either red (the first Americans) or black (the enslaved Americans). Ours is also an age in which dictators and demagogues have trampled on the basic rights of persons created in God's image solely because of their race, religion, or national origin. By witnessing boldly to the essential dignity and equality of all human beings under God, the church encourages the state to guarantee to all citizens equal justice under the civil law.

Just as the church plays an auxiliary role in connection with the struggles of the state for civil justice, so the state affects the work of the church insofar as it preserves the kind of open society in which the church can perform its divine mission. We will now review five of the chief ways in which the functional interaction of church and state works reciprocally to the church's benefit.

First, the state relates to the interests of the church by ensuring religious liberty for all. The state, of course, has absolutely no power over Christian freedom, that "glorious liberty of the children of God" into which persons in Christ are graciously liberated from bondage to the evil forces of sin, death, and the demonic (Rom. 8:21). That is a free gift of God which the state can neither enact nor repeal.

Religious liberty, on the other hand, is one of the inalienable rights of persons which a just state protects by law. It safeguards the right of the people of God to give public witness to their faith in churches, hospitals, homes, seminaries, and other institutions of mercy and learning. It also protects the rights of Christian citizens to propagate their faith through the spoken and written word. It is true that the church of Christ has been able to survive "underground" when tyrants have sought to stamp out the faith. But such a suffering community—stripped of all its liberty and institutional resources—is not able to make its total witness for Christ. A just state will facilitate the church's earthly mission by recognizing and protecting the rights of its members to gather together for corporate worship and service.

Second, the state relates to the interests of the church by acknowledging that human rights are not the creation of the state. The United States Supreme Court has affirmed that "we are a religious people whose institutions presuppose a Supreme Being" (*Zorach v. Clauson,* 1952). This long-standing tradition runs throughout American history from the credo in the Declaration of Independence that all men are "endowed by their Creator with certain inalienable rights" down to the recent addition to the Pledge of Allegiance that we are a nation "under God." All such public affirmations and mottoes are admittedly ceremonial and theologically minimal. They may even provide the unevangelical foundations for a dangerously self-righteous "civil religion." Under continued vigilance, however, they may still serve as effective restraints upon the introduction of a godless secularism as the unofficially "established" religion of the land. It remains the unique task of the Christian homes and churches of the nation to identify the "Supreme Being" of the state as the God and Father of our Lord Jesus Christ.

Third, the state relates to the interests of the church by maintaining an attitude of "wholesome neutrality" toward church bodies in the context of the religious pluralism of our culture.

Christians are not called to create a "Christian" state or to employ the compulsory power of the government to enforce the observance of Christian devotions (as in public school devotional Bible reading and prayers). Such attempts represent a confusion of the law of creation and the gospel of redemption, the rule of Caesar and the rule of Christ.

At the same time, it should never be forgotten that the civil realm of law and power is also a part of God's created order. All persons and rulers are subject to his sovereign will, whether they are Christians or not. The fact that the state discharges a secular function in God's dispensation should not blind us to its sacred basis and character. The church is in a far better position to be the body of Christ—and not merely a respectable prop for "the American way of life"—when the state limits itself strictly to its own divine mission of secular justice.

Fourth, the state relates to the interests of the church by providing incidental benefits on a nonpreferential basis in recognition of the church's civil services which are also of secular benefit to the community. The fact that the church helps to produce responsible citizens is very important for the state. The American and Canadian governments have never directly subsidized the church's primary work in Christian sanctification; they have always indirectly supported its incidental work in Christian citizenship.

On the one hand, the United States Supreme Court has said that the First Amendment forbids the state to pass any laws which "aid one religion, aid all religions, or prefer one religion over another." It has further declared that the government may not directly finance religious groups, must be neutral among religious bodies and in religious matters, and cannot force religion, religious instruction, or a religious observance on anyone (*Everson v. Board of Education,* 1952).

On the other hand, the Supreme Court has also recognized that a "common sense" view of separation means that the claims of both "non-establishment" and "free exercise" must be kept in fruitful tension as each new case is judged on its own merits. To quote the Court at its nondoctrinaire best, "The First

Amendment does not say that in every and all respects there shall be a separation of church and state. Rather it studiously defines the manner, the specific ways, in which there shall be no concert or union or dependency one on the other. That is the common sense of the matter" (*Zorach v. Clauson,* 1952).

In the decisions outlawing compulsory prayers and devotional Bible reading in the public schools, the Court went out of its way to stress that "other types of interdependence between religious and other public institutions" were not at issue here (*Schempp v. School District of Abington, Pa.,* 1963). Indeed, the several opinions in these cases support the conclusion that consistent with the concept of "wholesome neutrality," government may accommodate its laws and programs to meet the needs of religious liberty and to further the religious interests of the people, so long as it does not thereby involve itself unduly in religious matters. This suggests that government may properly provide for churches and chaplains at military establishments and penal institutions, for the appointment of legislative chaplains and the praying of invocational prayers in legislative chambers, for tax exemptions for churches along with other educational, charitable, and eleemosynary groups, for the nondevotional study of the Bible in public schools, and for nondiscriminatory aid in public welfare programs.

Fifth, the state relates to the interests of the church by providing financial aid on a nonpreferential basis to church agencies engaged in the performance of social services which are also of secular benefit to the community. There are a growing number of areas in which the modern welfare state and the church have a concurrent interest and common concern. These now center in the fields of health, education, and social welfare. Both the church and the state operate schools, colleges, hospitals, homes. As populations boom, problems grow, and costs soar, society is gradually assuming its communal responsibilities more directly by supporting many of the social functions performed earlier by the church.

The state is now willing to pay church agencies for many social services which are primarily of secular (rather than religious) benefit to the community, and which a welfare state would otherwise have to provide itself. Such payments present no legal difficulties in most Canadian provinces. Under the United States Constitution, payments to church agencies seem to be permissible as long as a statute passes certain tests.

In the dictum of the Supreme Court, "To withstand the structures of the establishment clause, there must be a secular legislative purpose and a primary effect that neither advances nor inhibits religion" (*Schempp v. School District of Abington, Pa., 1963*). In addition, the Court has decreed as unconstitutional any "excessive entanglement between government and religion." It has also warned that "political division along religious lines was one of the principle evils against which the First Amendment was intended to protect" (*Lemon v. Kurtzman* and *Earley v. DiCenso, 1971*).

Even where such state aid is constitutionally legal, however, it may not always be socially desirable or ethically advisable. The church and its agencies must therefore decide in each case (1) if the integrity of the church's witness requires that the church itself pay for a given service, or (2) if the church may accept funds from the state for such a service, or (3) if the church considers that a particular service is the peculiar responsibility of the state alone. Prudentially, of course, any institution of the church that is the recipient of such public funds must face the fact that it takes the risk of being subject to governmental direction if it becomes financially dependent upon governmental financing.

In summary, we have reaffirmed the "sacred secularity" of God's people as they worship, witness, and work in his world. We have advocated the institutional separation and functional interaction of church and state in the United States and Canada.

We have thereby rejected the position of an absolute separation of church and state in favor of a mutually beneficial relationship in which each institution contributes to the general welfare and the common good by remaining true to its own nature and task.

The proposed "ethical guidelines" are not offered as unattainable ideals, inflexible principles, or unbreakable rules and regulations. Our evangelical freedom permits no such moral casuistry or canon law. The guidelines are designed rather to provide the church with some helpful perspective and direction in its ongoing dialogue with the modern welfare state in our pluralistic society.

Epilogue:
The Cracked Bell

Philadelphia's Liberty Bell symbolizes the ideals of the American Revolution. On its base are inscribed the words of Lev. 25:10, "Proclaim liberty throughout all the land unto all the inhabitants thereof." Current biblical scholarship helps us to grasp the original meaning of a profound verse that is frequently misinterpreted by the uncritical defenders of America's civil religion.

In the Old Testament, these words were originally part of the regulations governing the Jubilee Year. After seven sabbatical years, on the fiftieth year, came the Year of Jubilee, named after the Hebrew word *"yobhel"* (ram's horn) which was to be blown in public proclamation. At that time all transferred land reverted to the original owner, preventing any property from being sold in perpetuity. The intention of the Jubilee legislation was to preserve the well-being of Israel as a people, by forbidding the accumulation of land in the hands of a few wealthy families while most of the poverty-stricken peasants would be doomed to a state of landless serfdom.

The theology of divine law supporting this time-limited legislation asserts that God is the ultimate owner of the land and its fruits. There is no absolute right of private property. We are God's responsible and accountable stewards, enjoying land and property as a loan from him.

Moreover, God requires us to use the land and its resources for the liberty of all and not just for a select few. We are created our brother's keeper so that "if your brother becomes poor, and cannot maintain himself with you, you shall maintain him" (Lev. 25:35). Our economic affairs are to be conducted in the presence of the God who is the champion of the poor and the oppressed and who wants us, through just laws and equitable policies, to "proclaim liberty throughout *all* the land unto *all* the inhabitants thereof."

Later in Israel the idea of the Jubilee Year was taken up and used metaphorically by the postexilic prophet who wrote Isaiah 56–66. In what was probably his prophetic commission, this unknown prophet announced an eschatological Jubilee, brought about by God's own gracious intervention in history. God himself will grant liberty to the oppressed and emancipation to those in bondage. He declared that the "year of the Lord's favor" will bring salvation to his people, and simultaneously it will be a "day of vengeance" for their oppressors (Isa. 61:1–2).

In the New Testament, Jesus preached his inaugural sermon in Nazareth's synagogue. In a scene which summarizes the whole message of the Third Gospel (Luke 4:16–30), it is of great significance that Jesus initiates his public ministry by reading from Isaiah's Jubilee message (Luke 4:18–19):

> The Spirit of the Lord is upon me, because he has anointed me to preach good news to the poor. He has sent me to proclaim release to the captives and recovering of sight to the blind, to set at liberty those who are oppressed, to proclaim the acceptable year of the Lord.

Jesus then went on to announce: "Today this scripture has been fulfilled." Later we find this same prophetic message proclaimed in the form of the Beatitudes (Luke 6:20–23). The Spirit-filled Messiah (Anointed One) brings that which sinful persons cannot and will not accomplish on the basis of the law. Our debts to God are canceled and our sins pardoned through the Savior who identified with publicans and sinners, accepted the cross, and who thereby established the glorious liberty of the children of God in the midst of a sin-enslaved world.

In short, the gospel is the good news that Jesus is the liberator of God who frees us from the bondage of sin and death (the messianic Jubilee). In grateful obedience, Christians serve God's universal law in alleviating human injustice and oppression (the economic Jubilee). As the messianic Jubilee announces God's merciful rule as our Redeemer, so the economic Jubilee witnesses to his sovereign governance as our Creator.

We are now compelled to ask how well we have lived out this liberating will of God in our time and in our land. To be sure, the Jubilee legislation as such is not legalistically binding on us. We are not ancient Jews living in the fifteenth or fifth century B.C. when such economic directives in nomadic or agricultural societies were likely a quite just expression of neighbor love.

It is immediately obvious that such decrees are no longer God's direct word to us in our modern industrialized societies. Especially in places where the sovereignty of God's law is rejected, Marxist communism has been able to abolish private property only at the cost of imposing military dictatorships on oppressed people. Returning all the American land to the Indians would hardly contribute to the total well-being of our two hundred million non-Indians.

Nevertheless, God's will for justice as expressed in the Jews' peculiar economic legislation remains as binding on us today as it was in Moses' time. All persons created in God's holy and loving image are to enjoy their fair share of the earth's resources, over which they have been called to exercise their own God-like (holy and loving) "dominion" (Gen. 1:26–28).

We Christians living in the United States must now confess that our liberty bell is badly cracked! We proclaim that Christ is the Bread of Life at the same time that most of humanity is hungry.

Our messianic Jubilee is not adequately governing our economic Jubilee. We are violating God's commission for us to care for his good earth through our sinful greed and avarice, our unjust laws and gross economic inequalities. Liberty is being proclaimed to only *some* of the inhabitants throughout only *some* of the land. "Starvation without representation!" is rapidly becoming a new revolutionary cry throughout the world.

Caring through sharing is the biblical answer for those of us

171

who believe that "the earth is the Lord's and the fulness thereof, the world and those who dwell therein" (Ps. 24:1). How can we enforce the demands of God's law against poverty through massive changes in our social legislation, tax structures, foreign development, and trade policies? How can we balance the claims of economic equality and political freedom? How can we distribute our wealth more fairly in celebration of the American dream of "liberty and justice for all"?

One helpful start might be for readers to complete this unfinished Bible study or sermon research as a part of their own personal commitment to the integration of Christian discipleship and American patriotism.